Modern Critical Interpretations

Vladimir Nabokov's
Lolita

Modern Critical Interpretations

These and other titles in preparation

Vladimir Nabokov's
Lolita

Edited and with an introduction by

Harold Bloom
Sterling Professor of the Humanities
Yale University

Chelsea House Publishers ◇ *1987*
NEW YORK ◇ NEW HAVEN ◇ PHILADELPHIA

© 1987 by Chelsea House Publishers, a division
of Chelsea House Educational Communications, Inc.,
  95 Madison Avenue, New York, NY 10016
  345 Whitney Avenue, New Haven, CT 06511
  5014 West Chester Pike, Edgemont, PA 19028

Introduction © 1987 by Harold Bloom

Printed and bound in the United States of America

∞ The paper used in this publication meets the minimum
requirements of the American National Standard for Permanence
of Paper for Printed Library Materials, Z39.48-1984.

Library of Congress Cataloging-in-Publication Data
Vladimir Nabokov's Lolita.
  (Modern critical interpretations)
  Bibliography: p.
  Includes index.
  1. Nabokov, Vladimir Vladimirovich, 1899–1977.
Lolita. I. Bloom, Harold. II. Series.
PS3527.A15L638 1987   813'.54   86–33454
ISBN 1–55546–040–2 (alk. paper)

Contents

Editor's Note

This book gathers together what seems to me a representative selection of the best criticism so far devoted to Vladimir Nabokov's novel, *Lolita*. The critical essays are reprinted here in the chronological order of their original publication. I am grateful to Shawn Rosenheim for his assistance in editing this volume.

My introduction joins in the universal appreciation of Nabokov as a stylist, while expressing some reservations as to his fictive insights, and suggesting that Freud wins an uncanny triumph over the virulently anti-Freudian Nabokov in the second part of *Lolita*.

The chronological sequence of criticism begins with Lionel Trilling's defense of *Lolita*, a defense that exalts Humbert Humbert as "the last lover," but one who exhibits also a "curious moral mobility." Morality is also Martin Green's concern in his account of *Lolita*, which contrasts Nabokov and Tolstoy on the ends of art.

Parody, Nabokov's major mode, is examined in *Lolita* by Alfred Appel, Jr., Nabokov's annotator and follower. Julia Bader reads *Lolita* as a parable of Nabokov's own aesthetic quest for ecstasy, a quest of which Humbert is both a mad representative and a complex travesty.

In an attempt to find and hold whatever middle ground *Lolita* can provide, Michael Bell argues that the book resists readings that would see it either as pure game or as moral vision. A subtler perspective is provided by Thomas R. Frosch, critic of Blake and Shelley, who discovers in *Lolita* the magic of the shaman, and reminds us that parody is one of the most powerful spells in a shaman's armory. In this book's final essay, David Rampton judges *Lolita* as a representation of "the human situation it portrays."

Introduction

Lolita, baroque and subtle, is a book written to be reread, but whether its continued force matches the intricacy of its design seems to me problematic. Little is gained for Nabokov by comparing him to Sterne or to Joyce. Borges, who was essentially a parodist, is an apter parallel to Nabokov. Perhaps parodists are fated to resent Sigmund Freud; certainly Borges and Nabokov are the modern writers who most consistently and ignorantly abuse Freud.

Where Nabokov hardly can be overpraised is in his achievement as a stylist. This is one of the endlessly dazzling paragraphs of *Lolita:*

> So Humbert the Cubus schemed and dreamed—and the red sun of desire and decision (the two things that create a live world) rose higher and higher, while upon a succession of balconies a succession of libertines, sparkling glass in hand, toasted the bliss of past and future nights. Then, figuratively speaking, I shattered the glass, and boldly imagined (for I was drunk on those visions by then and underrated the gentleness of my nature) how eventually I might blackmail—no, that is too strong a word—mauvemail big Haze into letting me consort with little Haze by gently threatening the poor doting Big Dove with desertion if she tried to bar me from playing with my legal stepdaughter. In a word, before such an Amazing Offer, before such a vastness and variety of vistas, I was as helpless as Adam at the preview of early oriental history, miraged in his apple orchard.

It is a grand prose-poem, and the entire book in little. Reading it aloud is a shocking pleasure, and analyzing it yet another pleasure, more inward and enduring. Humbert, more "cubus" than "incubus," casts the red sun of

1

his lustful will over the aptly named Haze females, yet avoids incurring our moral resentment by the exuberance of his language, with its zest for excess. What could be more captivating and memorable than: "while upon a succession of balconies a succession of libertines, sparkling glass in hand, toasted the bliss of past and future nights?" That delicious double "succession" achieves a kind of higher innocence, insouciant and stylized, delighting more in the language than in the actual possibility of sensual bliss. Shattering the sparkling glass, Humbert breaks the vessels of reverie in order to achieve a totally drunken vision of sexual exploitation, indeed like a new Adam overcome by the fumes of the fruit.

What Nabokov offers, in *Ada* as well as *Lolita*, is an almost pure revel in language, by no means necessarily allied with insight. His loathing of Freud reduces, I think, to a fear of meaning, to a need to defend against overdetermined sense, a sense that would extend to everything. Memory, in Nabokov, fears not so much Oedipal intensities as it does more-than-Oedipal genealogies. Here, Nabokov compares weakly to Proust, his most daunting precursor. *Lolita* gives us Marcel as Humbert and Albertine as Lolita, which is to replace a sublime temporal pathos by a parodistic cunning that unfortunately keeps reminding us how much we have lost when we turn from Proust to Nabokov.

II

Early defenses of *Lolita* by John Hollander and Lionel Trilling centered upon the insistence that it was an authentic love story. Rereading *Lolita* now, when no one would accuse the book of being pornography, I marvel that acute readers could take it as a portrayal of human love, since Humbert and Lolita are hardly representations of human beings. They are deliberate caricatures, as fabulistic as Charlotte Haze and Clare Quilty. Solipsistic nightmares, they wander in the America of highways and motels, but would be more at home in *Through the Looking-Glass* or *The Hunting of the Snark*. Poor Lolita indeed is a Snark, who precisely does not turn out to be a Boojum.

Nabokov, like Borges, is the most literary of fantasists, and takes from reality only what is already Nabokovian. Jane Austen, a powerful Protestant will, was as interested in social reality as the compulsive Dreiser was, but Nabokov's social reality died forever with the Bolshevik Revolution. Admirers who defend Nabokov's writing as mimesis do him violence. His genius was for distorted self-representation. Whether the Proustian intensities of sexual jealousy lend themselves to the phantasmagoric mode of

Gogol is a considerable question, but Nabokov intrepidly did not wait for an answer.

"So what is that queer world, glimpses of which we keep catching through the gaps of the harmless looking sentences. It is in a way the *real* one but it looks wildly absurd to us, accustomed as we are to the stage setting that screens it." That is Nabokov on Gogol, or Nabokov on Nabokov. It is not Humbert on Humbert. Nabokov's uncanny art refuses identification with his protagonist, yet lends the author's voice to the comically desperate pursuer of nymphets. "The science of nympholepsy is a precise science," says Humbert and we reflect that Nabokov is the scientist, rather than poor Humbert, a reflection that is proved by an even more famous declaration:

> I am not concerned with so-called "sex" at all. Anybody can imagine those elements of animality. A greater endeavor lures me on: to fix once for all the perilous magic of nymphets.

Humbert perhaps knows that "the perilous magic" of eroticism crosses animality with death; Nabokov certainly knows, though he rejects so crassly the greatest of modern knowers, Freud. Rejecting Freud however is not a possible option in our time, and the whole of Part Two of *Lolita* is an involuntary repetition of *Beyond the Pleasure Principle*. The death drive, fueled by that negative libido Freud once toyed with calling "destrudo," takes over poor Humbert completely, through the agency of his dark double and despoiler, Clare Quilty. Refusing to compound with Freud, who is the greatest and most pervasive of modern imaginations, Nabokov is doomed merely to repeat the Freudian mythology of the dual drives, Eros-Humbert and Thanatos-Quilty. All of Part Two of *Lolita* becomes, not a parody, but a Freudian allegory, considerably less splendid than the joyous Part One.

Humbert's murder of Quilty is at once the most curious and the least persuasive episode in *Lolita*. Each figure is the "familiar and innocuous hallucination" of the other, and Humbert's bungling execution of his double lifts the book momentarily into the category of nightmare. It is no accident that Humbert returns to the slain Quilty (C. Q.) in the novel's closing sentences:

> And do not pity C. Q. One had to choose between him and H. H., and one wanted H. H. to exist at least a couple of months longer, so as to have him make you live in the minds of later generations. I am thinking of aurochs and angels, the secret

>   of durable pigments, prophetic sonnets, the refuge of art. And
>   this is the only immortality you and I may share, my Lolita.

That doesn't *sound* to me like Humbert, and rather clearly Nabokov has usurped these closing tonalities, explaining why he did not have Quilty murder Humbert, which I suspect would have made a better end. I don't hear remoteness in this final tone, but rather an attempt to recover something of the aura of Part One, so sadly lost in the frenzies of Humbert's later sorrows.

The Last Lover:
Vladimir Nabokov's *Lolita*

Lionel Trilling

Lolita is about love. Perhaps I shall be better understood if I put the statement in this form: *Lolita* is not about sex, but about love. Almost every page sets forth some explicit erotic emotion or some overt erotic action and still it is not about sex. It is about love.

This makes it unique in my experience of contemporary novels. If our fiction gives accurate testimony, love has disappeared from the Western world, just as Denis de Rougemont said it should. The contemporary novel can tell us about sex, and about sexual communion, and about mutuality, and about the strong fine relationships that grow up between men and women; and it can tell us about marriage. But about love, which was once one of its chief preoccupations, it can tell us nothing at all.

My having mentioned Denis de Rougemont and his curious, belated, supererogatory onslaught on love will indicate that I have in mind what I seem to remember he calls passion-love, a kind of love with which European literature has dealt since time immemorial but with especial intensity since the Arthurian romances and the code of courtly love. Passion-love was a mode of feeling not available to everyone—the authorities on the subject restricted it to the aristocracy—but it was always of the greatest interest to almost everyone who was at all interested in the feelings, and it had a continuing influence on other kinds of love and on the literary conventions through which love was represented.

The essential condition of this kind of love was that it had nothing to do with marriage and could not possibly exist in marriage. Alanus Ca-

From *Speaking of Literature and Society*. © 1958 by Lionel Trilling, © 1980 by Diana Trilling and James Trilling. Harcourt Brace Jovanovich, Inc., 1980.

pellanus in his manual on courtly love set it down as perfectly obvious doctrine that a husband and wife cannot be lovers. The reason was that theirs was a practical and contractual relationship, having reference to estates and progeny. It was not a relation of the heart and the inclination, and the situation of the lady made it impossible for her to give herself in free will because it was expected that she give herself in obedience. That the possibility of love could exist only apart from and more or less in opposition to marriage has been, by and large, the traditional supposition of the European upper classes, which have placed most of their expectations of erotic pleasure outside of marriage.

It was surely one of the most interesting and important of cultural revisions when the middle classes, which had been quite specifically excluded from the pleasure and dignity of love (one cannot be both busy and a lover), began to appropriate the prestige of this mode of feeling and to change it in the process of adopting it. For they assimilated it to marriage itself, and required of married love that it have the high brilliance and significance of passion-love. Something of that expectation still persists—it is still the love poetry and the love music and the love dramas of passion-love in its later forms that shape our notions of what the erotic experience can be in intensity, in variety, in grace.

But inevitably the sexual revolution of our time brought the relationship between marriage and passion-love to a virtual end. Perhaps all that the two now have in common is the belief that the lovers must freely choose each other and that their choice has the highest sanctions and must not be interfered with. Apart from this, every aspect of the new relationship is a denial of the old ideal of love. If one can rely on the evidence of fiction to discover the modern idea of the right relation between a man and a woman, it would probably begin with a sexual meeting, more or less tentative or experimental, and go on to sexual communion, after which marriage would take place. There would follow a period in which husband and wife would each make an effort to get rid of their *merely symbolic* feelings for the other *partner* in the marriage and to learn to see each other *without illusion* and as they are *in reality*. To do this is the sign of *maturity*. It enables husband and wife to *build a life together*. In the *mutuality* and *warmth* of their *togetherness* their children are included. Towards each other, as towards their children, they show *tolerance* and *understanding,* which they find it easier to do if they have a *good sexual relationship*.

The condition towards which such a marriage aspires is *health*—a marriage is praised by being called a *healthy* marriage. This will suggest how far the modern ideal of love is from passion-love. The literal meaning of the word *passion* will indicate the distance. Nowadays we use the word chiefly to mean an intense feeling, forgetting the old distinction between a passion and an emotion, the former being an emotion before which we are helpless, which we have to *suffer,* in whose grip we are *passive.* The passion-lover was a sick man, a *patient.* It was the convention for him to say that he was sick and to make a show of his physical and mental derangement. And indeed by any modern standard of emotional health what he was expected to display in the way of obsessional conduct and masochism would make his condition deserve some sort of pretty grave name. His passion filled his whole mind to the exclusion of everything else; he submitted himself to his *mistress* as her *servant,* even her *slave,* he gloried in her *power* over him and expected that she would make him suffer, that she would be *cruel.*

Obviously I am dealing with a convention of literature, not describing the actual relationship between men and women. But it was a convention of a peculiar explicitness and force and it exerted an influence upon the management of the emotions down through the nineteenth century. At that time, it may be observed, the creative genius took over some of the characteristics of the lover: his obsessiveness, his masochism, his noble subservience to an ideal, and his antagonism to the social conventions, his propensity for making a scandal.

For scandal was of the essence of passion-love, which not only inverted the marital relationship of men and women but subverted marriage itself. It could also subvert a man's social responsibility, his honour. In either case, a scandal resulted, the extent of which measured the force of the love. Typically it led to disaster for the lovers, to death. For one aspect of the pathology of love was that it made of no account certain established judgments, denying the reality and the good of much in the world that is indeed real and good. In this respect lovers were conceived of much as we conceive of the artist—that is, as captivated by a reality and a good that are not of the ordinary world.

Now it may well be that all this is absurd, and really and truly a kind of pathology, and that we are much the better for being quite done with it, and that our contemporary love-ideal of a firm, tolerant, humorous, wry, happy marriage is a great advance from it. The world seems to be agreed that this is so—the evidence is to be found in a wide range of testimony from the most elementary fiction and the simplest handbook of marriage up to psychoanalysis and the works of D. H. Lawrence, for whom "love" was anathema. But the old ideal, as I have said, still has its charm for us—we still understand it in some degree; it still speaks to us of an intensity and grace of erotic emotion and behaviour that we do not want to admit is entirely beyond our reach.

If a novelist wanted, for whatever strange reason, to write a novel about the old kind of love, how would he go about it? How would he find or contrive the elements that make love possible?

For example, if love requires scandal, what could the novelist count on to constitute a scandal? Surely not—as I have already suggested—adultery. The very word is archaic; we recognise the possibility of its use only in law or in the past. Marital infidelity is not thought of as necessarily destructive of marriage, and, indeed, the word *unfaithful,* which once had so terrible a charge of meaning, begins to sound quaint, seeming to be inappropriate to our modern code. A few years ago William Barrett asked, *à propos* the effect of *Othello* on a modern audience, whether anyone nowadays could really comprehend and be interested in the spectacle of Othello's jealousy. I think that both comprehension and interest are possible. There are more than enough of the old feelings still left—nothing is ever thrown out of the attic of the mind—to permit us to understand perfectly well what Othello feels. Here we must be aware of the difference between life and literature. It is of course not true that people do not feel sexual jealousy; it is still one of the most intense of emotions. But they find it ever harder to believe that they are justified in feeling it, that they do right to give this emotion any authority. A contemporary writer would not be able to interest us in a situation like Othello's because, even if he had proof in his own experience of the actuality of jealousy, he could not give intellectual credence, or expect his readers to give it, to an emotion which in Shakespeare was visceral, questionable, of absolute authority.

But the breaking of the taboo about the sexual unavailability of very young girls has for us something of the force that a wife's infidelity had for Shakespeare. H. H.'s relation with Lolita defies society scandalously as did Tristan's relation with Iseult, or Vronsky's with Anna. It puts the lovers, as lovers in literature must be put, beyond the pale of society.

Then the novelist, if he is to maintain the right conditions for a story of passion-love, must see to it that his lovers do not approach the condition of marriage. That is, their behaviour to each other must not be touched by practicality, their virtues must not be of a kind that acknowledges the claims of the world. As soon as mutuality comes in, and common interests, and cooperation, and tolerance, and a concern for each other's welfare or prestige in the world, the ethos of the family, of marriage, has asserted itself and they lose their status of lovers. Their behaviour to each other must be precisely not what we call "mature"—they must see each other and the world with the imperious absolutism of children. So that a man in the grip of an obsessional lust and a girl of twelve make the ideal couple for a story about love written in our time. At least at the beginning of his love for

Lolita there are no practical moral considerations, no practical personal considerations, that qualify H. H.'s behaviour. As for Lolita, there is no possibility of her bringing the relation close to the condition of marriage because she cannot even imagine the female rôle in marriage. She remains perpetually the cruel mistress; even after her lover has won physical possession of her, she withholds the favour of her feeling, for she has none to give, by reason of her age, possibly by reason of her temperament.

Then the novelist must pay due attention to making the lover's obsession believable and not ridiculous. Nowadays we find it difficult to give credence to the idea that a man might feel that his reason and his very life depended on the response to him of a particular woman. Recently I read *Liber Amoris* with some graduate students and found that they had no understanding whatever of Hazlitt's obsessive commitment to Sarah Walker. They could see no reason why a man could not break the chains of a passion so unrewarding, so humiliating. I later regretted having been cross at their stupidity when I found myself doubting the verisimilitude of Proust's account of the relation of Swann to Odette. But our doubts are allayed if the obsession can be accounted for by the known fact of a sexual peculiarity, an avowed aberration. Pathology naturalises the strange particularity of the lover's preference.

I may seem to have been talking about *Lolita* as if in writing it Mr. Nabokov had undertaken a job of emotional archaeology. This may not be quite fair to Mr. Nabokov's whole intention, but it does suggest how regressive a book *Lolita* is, how, although it strikes all the most approved modern postures and attitudes, it is concerned to restore a foredone mode of feeling. And in nothing is *Lolita* so archaic as in its way of imaging the beloved. We with our modern latitude in these matters are likely to be amused by the minor details of his mistress's person that caught the lover's fancy in the novels of the nineteenth century—the expressiveness of the eyes, a certain kind of glance, a foot, an ankle, a wrist, an ear, a ringlet; with our modern reader's knowledge of the size and shape of the heroine's breasts, thighs, belly, and buttocks, these seem trifling and beside the point. Yet the interest in the not immediately erotic details of the female person was not forced on the lover or the novelist by narrow conventions; rather, it was an aspect of the fetishism which seems to attend passion-love, a sort of synecdoche of desire, in which the part stands for the whole, and even the glove or the scarf of the beloved has an erotic value. This is the mode of H. H.'s adoration of Lolita, and against the background of his sexual greed, which he calls "ape-like," it comes over us as another reason for being shocked, that in recent fiction no lover has thought of his beloved with so much tenderness, that no woman has been so charmingly evoked, in such grace and delicacy, as Lolita; the description of her tennis game, in which even her racket has an erotic charm, is one of the few examples of rapture in modern writing.

It seems to me that it is impossible to miss the *parti pris* in Mr. Nabokov's archaeological undertaking, the impulse to mock and discredit all forms of progressive rationalism not only because they are stupid in themselves but because they have brought the madness of love to an end. But Mr. Nabokov is not partisan to the point of being dishonest about the true nature of love. It is H. H., that mixture of ferocity and jocularity, who reminds us that "Love seeketh only self to please. . . . And builds a Hell in Heaven's despite." The passages in which Humbert gives voice to this judgment are not as well done as one might wish; they stand in an awkward relation to the tone and device of the book. Yet perhaps for that very reason they are the more startling and impressive (if we do not read them in a mood which makes them seem to verge upon the maudlin).

And in the end H. H. succumbs, and happily, to the dialectic of the history of love. I have represented passion-love as being the antithesis of marriage and as coming to an end when the conditions characteristic of marriage impose themselves, by whatever means, upon the lovers. Yet it is always to marriage that passion-love aspires, unique marriage, ideal marriage, marriage available to no other pair, but marriage nonetheless, with all the cramping vows and habitualness of marriage. And it is just this that H. H. eventually desires. Mr. Nabokov is, among his other accomplishments, an eminent entomologist and I shall leave it to some really rigorous close reader of fiction to tell us what an entomological novelist wants us to do with the fact that *nymph* is the name for the young of an insect without complete metamorphosis. Probably nothing. But he is also a scholar of languages and he knows that *nymph* is the Greek word for *bride*. He does not impart this information to us, yet he is at pains, as I have remarked, to put us in mind of the rapturous, tortured marriage of Poe and Virginia, and one of his last meditations on Lolita is of the constancy she evokes from him despite the ravages of time having destroyed the old incitements to lust:

> There she was with her ruined looks and her adult, rope-veined narrow hands and her gooseflesh white arms, and her shallow ears, and her unkempt armpits, there she was (my Lolita!), hopelessly worn at seventeen, with that baby, dreaming already in her of becoming a big shot and retiring around A.D. 2020— and I looked and looked at her, and knew as clearly as I know I

am to die, that I loved her more than anything I had ever seen or imagined on earth, or hoped for anywhere else. She was only the faint violet whiff and dead leaf echo of the nymphet I had rolled myself upon with such cries in the past; an echo on the brink of a russet ravine, with a far wood under a white sky, and brown leaves choking the brook and one last cricket in the crisp weeds . . . but thank God it was not that echo alone that I worshipped. What I used to pamper among the tangled vines of my heart, *mon grand péché radieux,* had dwindled in its essence: sterile and selfish vice, all *that* I cancelled and cursed. You may jeer at me, and threaten to clear the court, but until I am gagged and half-throttled, I will shout my poor truth. I insist the world know how much I loved my Lolita, *this* Lolita, pale and polluted, and big with another's child, but still grey-eyed, still sooty-lashed, still auburn and almond.

I am not sure just how I respond to the moral implication of this passage—I am not sure that with it, as with other passages in which H. H. speaks of the depth and wild solemnity of his love and remorse, Mr. Nabokov has not laid an emotional trap for the reader, that perhaps H. H.'s last intensities ought not to be received with considerably more irony than at first they call for. I don't say this with the least certitude. It may be that Mr. Nabokov really wants us to believe with entire seriousness that we are witnessing the culmination of H. H.'s moral evolution. Perhaps he even wants us to believe that his ascent from "ape-like" lust to a love which challenges the devils below and the angels up over the sea to ever dissever his soul from the soul of the lovely Annabel Lee constitutes the life cycle of the erotic instinct. I can, I think, manage to take seriously a tragic Humbert, but I find myself easier with Humbert the anti-hero, with Humbert as cousin-german to Rameau's nephew.

I don't want to put my uneasiness with the tragic Humbert as an objection. Indeed, for me one of the attractions of *Lolita* is its ambiguity of tone—which is pretty well exemplified in the passage I have quoted—and its ambiguity of intention, its ability to arouse uneasiness, to throw the reader off balance, to require him to change his stance and shift his position and move on. *Lolita* gives us no chance to settle and sink roots. Perhaps it is the curious moral mobility it urges on us that accounts for its remarkable ability to represent certain aspects of American life.

Tolstoy and Nabokov: The Morality of *Lolita*

Martin Green

People talk of the art of the future, meaning by art of the future some especially refined new art which they imagine will be developed out of that exclusive art of one class which is now considered the highest art. But no such new art of the future can or will be found.

Lev Tolstoy, *What Is Art?*

But the art of the twentieth century has been, by and large, of the kind Tolstoy declared would not—must not—happen. Nearly all our really brilliant literature, in Europe and America, has been of that kind and not of the kind *he* prescribed. And though there are many varieties within the huge body of modern art, the type Tolstoy would have most abominated, the type he was most talking about, is near enough epitomized in *Lolita*. This can be made clear in a direct way by referring to his descriptions of the literature he dislikes, and indirectly from those descriptions of what literature *should* be which occupy most of the space of *What Is Art?* He defined that "art of the future" which he announced *would* come by making it the opposite of all we find in Nabokov's work, which he can be said to have foretold quite accurately, by negation and by retrospect. And this is not such a paradox, nor such a wanton conjunction of the radically unrelated, as it may seem. Nabokov stands in immediate and intimate relationship to that symbolist tradition Tolstoy was denouncing, which replaced Tolstoy's own tradition in Russian literature. He belongs to that branch of the tradition sometimes called decadent; Sologub's *The Petty Demon,* for instance, has a good deal in common with *Lolita,* though it is incomparably less interesting.

From *The Kenyon Review* 28, no. 3 (June 1982). © 1966 by Kenyon College.

The special refinement of Nabokov's art is clear enough, both in the exquisite rendering of his effects and in the trickiness of those effects—the highly sophisticated taste they express, which so energetically avoids every suspicion of the ordinary, of the obvious, of the morally or intellectually banal. Who can compare with Nabokov for this refinement, among the writers who have appeared since *What Is Art?* was published? Not Lawrence, or Joyce, or Mann. For equal refinement we would have to go to a minor writer, or to other Russians, to other developers of that "exclusive art of one class," to Balanchine or to Stravinsky. Those three have among them contributed much of the most elegant art, of the most sophisticated taste, to the contemporary Western world; and behind them Fabergé, Diaghilev, the impressionist collections—all St. Petersburg still stands as a glittering emblem.

As Mirsky says in *Contemporary Russian Literature,* "Russian Symbolism is a part of the general cultural upheaval which changed the face of Russian civilization between 1890 and 1910. . . . In 1890 the sole function of art in Russia was to 'express ideas'; in 1915 Russian society was aesthetically one of the most cultivated and experienced in Europe." And since 1917 the benefits of that aesthetic refinement have spread far beyond the frontiers of Russia. The ballet of Balanchine, the music of Stravinsky, the novels of Nabokov—these are the best of that art of the connoisseur Tolstoy rejected in favor of an art of the common man; the art of the future, in which "Only those productions will be esteemed art which transmit feelings drawing men together in brotherly union, or such universal feelings as can unite all men." There *are* modern ballets, symphonies, novels which serve that ideal with some success, notably in Soviet Russia, but nothing could go more against it than the theatrical and luxurious art of the three great expatriates, in which the instincts of the virtuoso and the impresario are disciplined only by the taste of a cosmopolitan intellectual. And of the three it is Nabokov and *Lolita* who present the most four-square target to the aim of Tolstoy's destructive analysis.

> We think the feelings experienced by people of our day and our class are very important and varied; but in reality almost all the feelings of people of our class amount to but three very insignificant and simple feelings—the feeling of pride, the feeling of sexual desire, and the feeling of weariness of life. These three feelings, with their offshoots, form almost the sole subject matter of the art of the rich classes.

These categories do not fit Nabokov's subject matter *descriptively*—for instance, it is not a hero's weariness of life he treats, but the pain and horror inherent in all life—but *diagnostically* they do fit. Seen from Tolstoy's point of view, that is, *Lolita* clearly would seem to anyone to fit those categories with variations, to be recognizably a development from the art which fitted them exactly. Tolstoy mentions, as contemporary examples of the sexual theme, Rémy de Gourmont's *Les Chevaux de Diomède* ("every page contains lust-kindling descriptions"), Pierre Louys's *Aphrodite,* and Huysmans's *Certains.* "They are all the productions of people suffering from erotic mania." Humbert Humbert's nympholepsy clearly would seem to Tolstoy a recognizable development of that "normal" erotic mania.

Of the three conditions he thought necessary to successful art, individuality of feeling, clarity of expression, and sincerity, the last was much the most important to Tolstoy. "Sincere" in some sense of course applies to *Lolita,* but it is in a sophisticated and tricky sense, while the way Tolstoy used the term made its simpler senses determinative. This condition, he says, "is always complied with in peasant art, and this explains why such art always acts so powerfully; but it is a condition almost entirely absent from our upper-class art, which is continually produced by artists actuated by personal aims of covetousness or vanity." With this kind of sincerity *Lolita* is not sincere. That folk-tale anonymity of the author, that austere elimination of all personal cleverness, is at the opposite extreme from the novel's art. Nor is it *clear; Lolita* obviously belongs to the "involved, affected, and obscure" genres typical of upper-class art. This art, Tolstoy said, because it came out of unbelief, had long ceased to aim at communicating with all men. It restricted itself to an "exclusive" audience, with whom it could communicate by "allusions comprehensible only to the initiated." This method had reached its climax (at the date of *What Is Art?*) in the work of the decadents. "It has finally come to this: that not only are haziness, mysteriousness, obscurity, and exclusiveness (shutting out the masses) elevated to the rank of merit and a condition of poetic art, but even inaccuracy, indefiniteness, and lack of eloquence, are held in esteem." The artistic tradition to which Tolstoy wished to attach himself, and which he wished to revive, was the narratively and morally simple tradition of the people: "the epic of Genesis, the Gospel parables, folk legends, fairy tales, and folk songs, are understood by all."

The function of art, said Tolstoy, is to aid human progress by spreading better feelings, just as the function of knowledge is to spread better ideas. "And as the evolution of knowledge proceeds by truer and more necessary knowledge dislodging and replacing what was mistaken and unnecessary, so the evolution of feeling proceeds by means of art—feelings less kind and less necessary for the well-being of mankind being replaced by others kinder and more needful for that end. That is the purpose of art." Art essentially unites people. It unites the reader with the writer, and with all the other readers, in sharing a more or less powerful impression and complex of feelings. The art of the future will be of two kinds, according to the two kinds of feeling it unites us in: "first, feelings flowing from a perception of our sonship to God and of the brotherhood of man; and next, the simple feelings of common life accessible to every one without exception—such as feelings of merriment, of pity, of cheerfulness, of tranquillity, and so forth." This is, phrased in simplistic, pamphleteering terms, part of the cultural theory of art in which many of us who admire *Lolita* were trained and still believe. But morally powerful as that program may still seem, it is plain that Nabokov's art devotes great energy to doing something quite the opposite. If we needed proof, we would find it in the examples Tolstoy gives from nineteenth-century literature of the first kind of art: Schiller's *The Robbers,* Hugo's *Les Misérables* and *Les Pauvres gens,* Dickens and Dostoyevski complete, *Uncle Tom's Cabin* and *Adam Bede.* The art of the second kind of feelings he could find no satisfactory examples of. While among those he condemns we find at least one whose example runs through *Lolita* as a kind of sponsor and precursor—Baudelaire. Nabokov's other sponsors of theme and expression, like Proust and T. S. Eliot, would have seemed hardly any better to Tolstoy.

Chapter 11 of *What Is Art?* is devoted to the methods of counterfeit art, which replaces true art when sincerity has failed. Those methods it calls borrowing, imitating, striking, and interesting. Borrowing means using previously established poetic subjects, setting, characters, or plot. Imitating means detailed descriptive realism. (*Lolita's* narrative manner can be described as an ingenious combination of those two.) Striking means directly affecting the senses. Interesting means with a subject of independent interest—like nympholepsy, for instance. Tolstoy did not say that these methods are incompatible with true art, but that they are irrelevant to it, and often a substitute for it.

Nabokov borrows, imitates, etc., a great deal, and that borrowing is far from irrelevant to his essential meaning. His meaning comes through his borrowing—through what is borrowed and also through the fact that it is borrowed. *Lolita* is fundamentally a counterfeit book, fundamentally not sincere as Tolstoy used that term, fundamentally tricky. The voice of the narrator, for instance, though ultimately quite moving and moved, quite committed on the book's basic issues, and therein simple, solid, direct, is all these things only after, and through, a great deal that is the opposite. We have a hundred reasons to distrust that voice. He is a murderer and a pervert. He is a dissenter from even the highest norms of thought and feeling. He is ironic and cynical—not only in his thoughts (about Charlotte) but in his actions (to Valeria). All this is true of his character alone, as established by the events he narrates. But something more fundamental is to be doubted and distrusted—his existence. Whoever writes the foreword, signed John Ray, Jr., Ph.D., is obviously the same person who signs himself Humbert Humbert. We recognize the same flow of overelegant language, always shifting (swelling absurdly, halting abruptly, changing its brand of elegance) in response to an acute sense of (taste in) its own glossy falsity. "If, however, for this paradoxical prude's comfort, an editor attempted to dilute or omit scenes that a certain type of mind might call 'aphrodisiac' . . ." This is the main voice of the novel, whatever it may sign itself, and to realize that this trick is being played on him rouses all a reader's distrust—of a gamesmanship kind.

But John Ray we can forget. Clare Quilty is rooted in the action of the novel, and it is much more deeply disturbing to recognize the hints that he too is unreal; that he and Humbert are two parts of the same personality. The similarity of their mental habits and sexual tastes, the differentiation between their moral guilts, the hallucinatory atmosphere of their encounters, the cousinly and indeed brotherly relationship foisted on them—by all these hints we are invited to believe that Humbert first invents Quilty, to take on the worst of his own guilt, and then kills him, to purge himself symbolically. But, if this is true, then a great many of the novel's events must be untrue, and the whole persona of the narrator is one we cannot take at face value.

Indeed, his very physique changes as the novel proceeds. At the beginning he is beetle-browed, pseudo-Celtic, intensely virile, "lanky, big-boned, woolly-chested," "a hunk of movieland manhood" with "clean-cut jaw, muscular hand, deep sonorous voice, broad shoulder." By the time he visits Lolita married, he is "the distant, elegant, slender, 40 year old valetudinarian in a velvet coat sitting beside her," and, "The men looked at her fragile, *frileux,* diminutive, old-world, youngish but sickly, father in velvet coat and beige vest, maybe a viscount." The more virile characteristics have been transferred to Lolita's husband—the blue eyes and black hair, the white teeth, the brawny shoulders and muscular arms. Richard Schiller is the final inheritor of several normal men (for instance, big Frank in Elphinstone) who have been contrasted with Humbert to his disadvantage through the second half of the book. Clearly, Humbert's original entity has again been split up, and the parts distributed among different actors, to dramatize an internal movement of self-hatred and self-punishment. The reader has to ask himself whether it is Humbert or Nabokov who does this—whether we can distinguish between what is invented by this narrator and what is reported—and the answer is complicated. The reader has to deal with a highly sophisticated reading experience, which challenges his assumption that he "knows what is going on" in matters of moral fundamentals as well as of narrative techniques.

And the voice itself, its handling of the language, amplifies all these effects. The tone is always at least double:

> My very photogenic mother died in a freak accident (picnic, lightning) when I was three, and, save for a pocket of warmth in the darkest part, nothing of her subsists within the hollows and dells of memory, over which, if you can still stand my style (I am writing under observation), the sun of my infancy had set; surely, you all know those redolent remnants of day suspended, with the midges, about some hedge in bloom or suddenly entered and traversed by the rambler, at the bottom of a hill, in the summer dusk; a furry warmth, golden midges.

Here let us note the abrupt change of rhythm in the first parenthesis; the mocking acknowledgment of his own overelegance—we have already been told to count on a murderer for a fancy prose style; and above all the sudden flowering of the image, at the end of the sentence, into something full-blown and beautiful, the reference of which is by no means clear, and the force of which alters the emotional balance and direction of the whole statement. We have to follow such syntax very carefully.

We have to follow the *narrative* very carefully, because so much is conveyed by allusion and ellipsis. The book is in part a game the narrator is playing against us (touché, reader, he says at one point), and he is not above cheating. He will tell us Lolita had gone forever, when in fact he merely felt then as if she had, and five lines later she is back. He will put Humbert and Valeria into an anonymous taxi, to discuss Valeria's infidelity, and then spotlight the taxi driver as her beloved. He will ascribe speeches and actions to people out of the exuberance of his own fancy. Sometimes he admits this afterward, as in the case of Charlotte's letter. Sometimes he does not, as in Humbert's absurdly pompous warning about reformatories to Lolita, or in Lolita's letter home, beginning "Dear Mummy and Hummy." This narrator is clearly someone both master and servant of his own taste for brilliant language. Anything vivid enough to demand to be said he will say, and retrieve his sincerity later—will temporarily throw away his identity and his serious purposes for an effect. And our instinct that this characteristic must run very deep in the sensibility of which Humbert is the spokesman is corroborated in "Vladimir Nabokov on a book entitled *Lolita*":

> After doing my impersonation of suave John Ray, the character in
> *Lolita* who pens the Foreword, any comments coming straight
> from me may strike one—may strike me, in fact—as an imper-
> sonation of Vladimir Nabokov talking about his own book. A
> few points, however, have to be discussed; and the auto-
> biographic device may induce mimic and model to blend.

Autobiography is a device, and to speak in his own voice is a matter of
having a model and being a mimic. With Nabokov there is always a mask,
and of a self-proclaiming kind. Sincerity is something he achieves not by
laying all masks aside but by manipulating them.

His private tragedy, he tells us there, is that he had to give up his native
language for "a second-rate brand of English, devoid of any of those apparatuses—the baffling mirror, the black velvet backdrop, the implied associations and traditions—which the native illusionist, frac-tails flying, can
use to transcend the heritage in his own way." This is in itself a tricky
statement, for none of our native illusionists has in fact used more of those
apparatuses, and few readers would say *Lolita* could be improved by *more*
baffling mirrors and black velvet backdrops. But the important point is
what is implied in the word illusionist, which is essential to what Nabokov
means by an artist, and essentially not what Tolstoy meant—a man of
tricks.

Tolstoy's examples of true art may seem at first remote from modern
practice; the stories of Isaac, Jacob, and Joseph, the Psalms and parables, the
Vedas, Homer, and the story of Sakyamuni. But the artistic virtues such a
selection is built around are obvious. Cardinal among them, perhaps, are
the artist's dignity and simplicity, the loftiness of his message and the plain-
ness of his manner. And if we look for more modern equivalents within our
own traditions, and for artist-figures to associate with such art, we find
them easily enough, in Emerson and Wordsworth, and in the later Tolstoy
himself. Indeed, the ideal he there sketches out is only an extreme version of
something everyone is familiar with in British literature; George Eliot,
Carlyle, Ruskin, Morris are all figures modeled after the same ideal to some
degree. They employed their gift of eloquence to proclaim noble truths
with noble gestures. It is Nabokov's version of the artist figure, as enigma
and paradox, which is really alien to our tradition.

> You have to be an artist and a madman, a creature of infinite
> melancholy, with a bubble of hot poison in your loins and a
> super-voluptuous flame permanently aglow in your subtle spine
> (oh, how you have to cringe and hide!), in order to discern at

once, by ineffable signs—the sightly feline outline of a cheek-
bone, the slenderness of a downy limb, and other indices which
despair and shame and tears of tenderness forbid me to tabu-
late—the little deadly demon among the wholesome children;
she stands unrecognized by them and unconscious herself of her
fantastic power.

The image of the illusionist is blended with the image of the madman and
the immoralist. Quilty, not Humbert, is a professional artist. Art is the
realm of both the theatrical and the delirious illusion; of the exaggerated, the
pretended, the masked, the suggested, the shameful, the feverish, the insane. It deals in truths that are banished from the open air and the daylight
and the world of self-respect, truths that have the status only of half-truths
or lies, because they cannot be fully faced or frankly stated. And the
methods of this art, the gestures of this artist-figure, are appropriate to its
subject matter. There can be no question of noble simplicity or plain direct-
ness.

Hence the artifice: the diary entries, the addresses to the jury, the staged
scenes, the painted pictures, and all the thousand devices of fantasy and
memory. They are intended to change the truth away from literalness.
"The arabesques of lighted windows, which, touched up by the coloured
inks of sensitive memory, appear to me now like playing cards—presumably because a bridge game was keeping the enemy busy." Hence, too,
those messages in the text of *Lolita* for people other than the reader—for the
printer, for the editor, for Lolita, for his lawyer, for his car, for Gaston
Godin—which yet are also for the reader, involving him in an artificial
complicity. There is that wealth of literary and linguistic reference, in-
dulged in partly for its own sake, and as a game. There are the French and
the German and the mock-Latin, and there is the constant refrain of references to Carmen and to Catullus and to Poe and to Dante. Related, there is
the game with names and titles—Lolita's class list, and the entries from
Who's Who in the Limelight. The climax of all this is the system of clues
Quilty scatters over the motels' visitors' books. Nabokov is playing with
words all through the book, and though his games are organic parts of the
action (partly because of Humbert's trickiness of character and characterization) they are so only through being games in and for themselves. They *are*
personal displays of cleverness on the writer's part; they *are* what Tolstoy
called the marks of bad art.

The poem, "Wanted, wanted, Dolores Haze," is an example of another
kind of trickiness in the novel. Humbert calls it a maniac's masterpiece, but,
though the rhymes are, as he says, "stark, stiff, lurid," the spirit of their

stiffness is not at all insane. Their spirit is comic-pathetic, and its tactics are most sane and sophisticated, the "unintentional" effects amplifying the intentional ones both in the wit and in the pathos:

> Where are you riding, Dolores Haze?
> What make is the magic carpet?
> Is a Cream Cougar the present craze?
> And where are you parked, my car pet?

If we call the second line an intentional effect of wit, then the clumsiness of the third is "unintentional" (a guarantee of sincerity), and the fourth is of course both.

> My car is limping, Dolores Haze,
> And the last long lap is the hardest,
> And I shall be dumped where the weed decays,
> And the rest is rust and stardust.

Here those two kinds of effect are less easily separated, and what we are more aware of is two kinds of parody; the first which deflates emotion, the second which inflates it, by making the mockery self-mockery—mockery of expression, that is, and a Romantic inflation of the inexpressible experience. Thus, the last phrase expands and asserts the poet's emotion—emotionally. This is typical of much of the writing in the novel, which appeals to our pity, our understanding, our delight, our liking for the hero, after seeming denials and devaluations of those feelings.

In all these ways, *Lolita* is a tricky novel, involving the reader in very risky games, many of the moves of which, and the counters of which, carry a high moral voltage. Neither narratively nor morally is it simple. And, at the root of all these differences between the prescriptions of *What Is Art?* and the texture and structure of *Lolita,* there is a sharp opposition of aesthetic theories. Tolstoy saw art as a matter of communication. "Art is a human activity consisting in this, that one man consciously by means of certain external signs, hands on to others feelings he has lived through, and that others are infected by these feelings and also experience them." And therefore good art is that kind which communicates good feelings. He completely rejected the ideal of beauty itself, and the giving of pleasure, as the ends of art. He thought such theories merely rationalized the aesthetic interests of an idle and irreligious upper class:

> So these people remained without any religious view of life; and
> having none, they could have no standard whereby to estimate
> what was good and what was bad art, except that of personal

enjoyment. And having acknowledged their criterion of what was good to be pleasure, that is beauty, these people of the upper classes of European society went back in their comprehension of art to the gross conception of the primitive Greeks, which Plato had already condemned. And conformably to this understanding of life a theory of art was formulated.

Nabokov's position is the opposite. Beauty and pleasure, fused into "aesthetic bliss," is art's only end and justification.

I am neither a reader nor a writer of didactic fiction, and despite John Ray's assertion, *Lolita* has no moral in tow. For me a work of fiction exists only insofar as it affords me what I shall bluntly call aesthetic bliss, that is a sense of being somehow, somewhere, connected with other states of being where art (curiosity, tenderness, kindness, ecstasy) is the norm.

That is by no means an easy sentence to read, but for the moment let us only note the diametrical opposition to Tolstoy. Humbert is even clearer in his rejection of every religious and moral scheme, every ideological synthesis within which art might have some function of cultural service:

Alas, I was unable to transcend the simple human fact that whatever spiritual solace I might find, whatever lithophanic eternities might be provided for me, nothing could make my Lolita forget the foul lust I had inflicted upon her. Unless it can be proven to me—to me as I am now, today, with my heart and my beard, and my putrefaction—that in the infinite run it does not matter a jot that a North American girl-child named Dolores Haze had been deprived of her childhood by a maniac, unless this can be proven (and if it can, then life is a joke) I see nothing for the treatment of my misery but the melancholy and very local palliative of articulate art. To quote an old poet:

> The moral sense in mortals is the duty
> We have to pay on mortal sense of beauty.

Religion, and *any* explanatory scheme, does not take human experience seriously enough. Only an attitude of protest and rage, refusing explanations, does. So art is superior to religion just because it *is* a melancholy and local palliative. *Lolita* is written as a melancholy and futile reparation to its heroine—"[to] make you live in the minds of later generations. I am thinking of aurochs and angels, the secret of durable pigments, prophetic sonnets, the refuge of art. And this is the only immortality you and I may share, my Lolita." The consolations of religion and the rigors of morality are both derived from the aesthetic sense. What is beautiful is so because it satisfies our moral sense among other things, but the idea of beauty is the larger. The moral sense is an obligation, which we pay resignedly as a part of the price of beauty. This duty is not Kantianly near to religion; it is nearer to Customs and Excise.

The interest of putting Nabokov and Tolstoy together at this length is not that they are different, for that would be conceded after a sentence, but that they are so very different. They represent opposite standards. Tolstoy's standard is so extreme that divergence from it seems only natural, yet Nabokov's opposition to it is so defiant that we must recognize *Lolita* as much more than an ordinary divergence. Putting them together, that is, brings out something in the morality of *Lolita* which does trouble us. Nabokov so flies in the face of all ordinary usable morality, and so defiantly offers us pieces of beauty as his justification for doing so, that some of us are bound to be uneasy. The readers I am assuming are people not prepared to take up either Tolstoy's position or its opposite—some equally stringent exposition of Nabokov's aesthetic bliss. We stand somewhere between the two. There is, for people in that position, surely some force to Tolstoy's account of the duties and accomplishments of art, or at least to the contrast between them and what Nabokov makes art do:

> All that now, independently of the fear of violence and punishment, makes the social life of man possible (and already this is an enormous part of the order of our lives)—all this has been brought about by art. If by art it has been inculcated upon people how they should treat religious objects, their parents, their children, their wives, their relations, strangers, foreigners; how to conduct themselves towards their elders, their superiors, towards those who suffer, towards their enemies, and towards animals; and if this has been obeyed through generations by millions of people, not only unenforced by any violence but so that the force of such customs can be shaken in no way but by means of art: then by art also other customs more in accord with the religious perceptions of our time may be evoked.

This is the task Tolstoy assigned to the art of the future. Though his phrasing is too moralistic to serve as a direct imperative to imaginative writers, still even Western literature since Tolstoy's time has contributed to that task in its own way and to some degree. A case like Lawrence's needs no arguing, but even Joyce's *Ulysses* offers us, in the figure of Bloom, a representation of "our fellow man" and "our common humanity" brought before us with a most loving intelligence and a most intelligent love. Nabokov stands, in the group of significant Western writers, fairly far out in the direction of freedom from all cultural-moral imperatives, in the direction of rejecting that task.

At the same time, when we compare that group as a whole with the equivalent group of Soviet writers, or with nineteenth-century writers, we see that the direction is what has characterized modern Western literature. So that Nabokov, from this point of view, may be said to represent all our writers, and his case has a representative significance. The Soviet writers have on the whole obeyed Tolstoy's prescriptions, and followed his view of the social function of art, and of aesthetics as a whole. Soviet literature is Tolstoy's "art of the future." Our literature is definitely not—is closer to being that development of upper-class exclusive art which he deplored— and though we may on the whole congratulate ourselves on the difference, some kinds of uneasiness persist, and are likely to be most acute when we are reading *Lolita*. *Is* this not after all an immoral book—for the way it flouts all cultural responsibility, not merely sexual decency? *Is* it not in fact the product of a corrupt culture—unbelieving, pleasure-seeking, beauty-worshiping? *Is* not Tolstoy ultimately right, at least about *Lolita* and everything like it?

Before attempting a moral defense of the book we should perhaps try to formulate the charge against it more in terms of its own imaginative life. The sexually perverse enterprises of the main character are made funny, beautiful, pathetic, romantic, tragic; in five or six ways we are made to sympathize with him in them. Above all, they are made impressive. When the poem begins, "Wanted, wanted, Dolores Haze," the pun in the first word has a great deal of power in it, for to want someone, in that sense, is a major fact, even an achievement, in modern literature, in modern culture. Sexual love is a major mythical form of human relationship, and all its pains and pleasures are taken seriously. Moreover, our novels are full of figures who are not able to want each other, or not able to want her or him fully— wanting is an achievement not to be taken for granted. Humbert, we are convinced, does want Lolita fully; he does love her. It is a perverse love, but it is love, and so is to be sympathized with. The novel thus breaks down one of our most intimate and powerful taboos. And the perversity involves Humbert necessarily in other kinds of immoral behavior—his manipulative marriages, for instance, and his cruel abduction of the child—with which again we are made to sympathize, to participate imaginatively, against our whole moral heritage.

But the sexual perversity gets its full flavor in the book from being type and symbol of a more general perversity; a rebellion against all morality. This rebellion is not harsh or loud; it is humorous, ironic, nonchalant, like most of Humbert's general attitudes; but it is profound. His habitual skepticism about all ordinary moral affirmations is ingrained in the prose. Such prose cannot be made to express affirmations. What it does express, and more naturally, more vividly, more consummately than anyone else's prose, is immoralism:

> I remember once handling an automatic belonging to a fellow student, in the days (I have not spoken of them, I think, but never mind) when I toyed with the idea of enjoying his little sister, a most diaphanous nymphet with a black hair bow, and then shooting myself. I now wondered if Valechka (as the colonel called her) was really worth shooting, or strangling, or drowning. She had very vulnerable legs, and I decided I would limit myself to hurting her very horribly as soon as we were alone.

It is the gaiety and the nonchalance as much as the substance of the statement which affront our moral sensibility. And the fact that this was a *friend*'s sister he though of "enjoying," and the friend's gun with which he would then shoot himself, shows the ingenuity with which Humbert's mind works out such affronts.

Then his actual treatment of Valeria, and later of Charlotte, is both cruel in itself and callously indifferent to our response. His sensibility as a whole is inspired by feeling of exasperation, offense at life, and revenge desired. Take for instance the very funny description of the night noises in the Enchanted Hunters hotel. The humor derives from an experience of acute exasperation, and one which fits into a habit of exasperation, one which gives the keynote to a whole range of feelings. Much of the motel-name humor is quite serenely and freely playful, but most of Humbert's wit derives from an impatience so sharp it has cut itself off from all sympathy with its object. This is the essence of the cruelty we feel in him toward Valeria and Charlotte. It expresses itself again in his feud with psychiatrists, in his gratuitous insults to Dr. Quilty and Mrs. Chatfield at the end of the book, and in his final driving down the wrong side of the road. Of the impulse to do this, he tells us, "In a way, it was a very spiritual itch." And indeed behind this impatience, this self-insulation, this radical alienation does lie something spiritual; a whole sense of himself as a changeling, in disguise, not fully human. He speaks often of his adult male disguise, but it is also a matter of his foreignness, of his other languages, of his hidden history. Nobody knows him as he really is. Of course, we must not make too much of this. Nabokov has made practically nothing. But Humbert clearly *is* an outsider in the fullest sense, and his sexual perversity is not an unfortunate accident. It is both the root and the emblem of his whole personality. We are being asked to make a hero out of someone in full-scale rebellion against whole systems of our moral inheritance.

And, finally, the tone and form of the novel, while they win our sympathy for Humbert, prevent that sympathy from following any conventional outlines of pity and understanding. The wit is insolent, the mockery is triumphant, and Humbert's irony is everywhere in the book. There is no vantage point from which to see beyond and around him. He has been beforehand with us in every tone to take about him. We are forced to succumb to his way of seeing himself and talking about himself.

We do all this at considerable cost to our self-respect and considerable moral mortification, if not debilitation. If all we get in return is a series of very funny incidents and passages of very beautiful writing, then we are likely to react with an unconscious resistance which will cramp the roots of that initial response. We should then be left, as many readers are who are not conscious of having made a moral judgment, with an experience of a clever and amusing novel which we can relegate without trouble to an unimportant literary category. If that is not to happen, we must find a powerful and (since so well-hidden) quite elaborate moral strategy within the novel.

That strategy can, I think, be described as a series of concessions, a self-criticism, a self-defense, and a moral theory of art. The major concession is making Lolita sexually experienced before she meets Humbert, and having her seduce him. This is right for the novel in several ways, but one most important way is as a concession to the reader's outraged sensibility, an easing of his act of sympathy with Humbert. Let Lolita be entirely innocent, and our feelings about the story would be very different. There are other concessions of the same kind, but let us pass immediately to another kind. In that disturbing episode of Valeria's confession, and particularly in the callous cruelty of Humbert's response, the narration enacts a comic criticism of him. It comments on his vanity; it exaggerates his complacency; it mocks his sense of superiority and security. In effect, we *are* here given a point of vantage from which to see beyond and around Humbert; we are allowed some relief from the effort of identifying ourselves with him. And there are other examples of this kind of concession, too.

But the problem, the challenge, is merely shaped by these concessions. Its resolution is a matter of the self-criticism, the self-defense, and the theory of art. Humbert criticizes himself, indeed hates himself, with an intensity which may perhaps escape our attention at first reading. Its expression is most often unobtrusively placed in the narrative; as for instance in the phrase "and my putrefaction" in the quoted sentence beginning, "Unless it can be proven to me"; or as in this, "But instead I am lanky, big-boned, woolly-chested Humbert Humbert, with thick black eyebrows and a queer accent, and a cesspoolful of rotting monsters behind his slow boyish smile." This unobtrusiveness becomes all the more telling as a mode of expression when such remarks are put together with that self-alienation discussed before—note "*his* slow boyish smile"—that poisoning of Humbert's sense of himself. And the counterpart to this is the overwhelming emotionalism, the desire to drown all consciousness in tears which wells up from time to time. "Oh let me be mawkish for the nonce! I am so tired of being cynical." This is most overt at key moments, such as the end of part one: "At the hotel we had separate rooms, but in the middle of the night she came sobbing into mine, and we made it up very gently. You see, she had absolutely nowhere else to go." But this note too recurs unobtrusively and obliquely throughout. In the middle of the gay description of the motels, we find, "And sometimes trains would cry in the monstrously hot and humid night with heartrending and ominous plangency, mingling power and hysteria in one desperate scream." *Lolita* remains a comic novel, but within the conventions of comedy Humbert is placed for us quite unequivocally, and with a strong sense of horror as well as pity. This horror is what is worked out in terms of plot and characterization by that splitting off of Quilty from Humbert discussed before, and by the killing of Quilty.

But that self-criticism, however unequivocal, is still not satisfyingly prominent in the novel. It is not in any sense the point of the characterization. More important than that is what I have called the self-defense, which is really an involvement of the reader with the hero, a binding together of the two. Humbert Humbert is our protagonist, and we are unable to dissociate ourselves from him self-righteously, because he represents a part of ourselves we are normally proud of. What he represents is, among other things, our intelligence. Humbert is one of the cleverest of novel heroes. His wit is brilliant, his observation ranges over everything, his taste is marvelously alive. When he does so callously make fun of Charlotte and Valeria, he carries us with him intellectually. We feel that they are funny, not just that he is being funny about them, even though we protest that we don't want to laugh. He is ourselves, without our inhibitions, acting out our tendencies. But, if so, then we cannot take the moral problems involved lightly; we are bound to undergo them painfully; to the extent that we are identified with Humbert, *Lolita* is a serious novel.

And he is even more importantly our protagonist in the matter of love.

That Humbert manages to love Lolita makes a powerful claim on our respect. He knows her completely, and he loves her completely, sensually and sentimentally and for herself, all at the same time. And he does so in that tradition of romantic love which is so important in our culture. Humbert loves Lolita in the way that Dante loved Beatrice, the way Petrarch loved Laura, the way Poe loved Virginia, the way Don José loved Carmen. The references to these great, tragic, idealistic love affairs run through the novel and challenge us to deny that Humbert's feelings belong to the same family and deserve the same respect.

Here he remembers his excitement at seeing (he mistakenly thought) a nymphet undressing at an opposite window:

> There was in the fiery phantasm a perfection which made my wild delight also perfect, just because the vision was out of reach, with no possibility of attainment to spoil it by the awareness of an appended taboo; indeed, it may well be that the very attraction immaturity has for me lies not so much in the limpidity of pure young forbidden fairy child beauty as in the security of a situation where infinite perfections fill the gap between the little given and the great promised—the great rosegray never-to-be-had.

This is, despite the irony of the occasion, one of the great minor chords in the symphony of romantic love; and the great major chord is this:

> She was only the faint violet whiff and dead leaf echo of the nymphet I had rolled myself upon with such cries in the past; an echo on the brink of a russet ravine, with a far wood under a white sky, and brown leaves choking the brook, and one last cricket in the crisp weeds . . . but thank God it was not that echo alone that I worshipped. What I used to pamper among the twisted vines of my heart, *mon grand péché radieux,* had dwindled to its essence: sterile and selfish vice, all *that* I canceled and cursed. You may jeer at me, and threaten to clear the court, but until I am gagged and half-throttled, I will shout my poor truth. I insist the world know how much I loved my Lolita, *this* Lolita, pale and polluted, and big with another's child, but still gray-eyed, still sooty-lashed, still auburn and almond, still Carmencita, still mine; *Changeons de vie, ma Carmen, allons vivre quelque part où nous ne serons jamais séparés;* Ohio? The wilds of Massachusetts? No matter, even if those eyes of hers would fade to myopic fish, and her nipples swell and crack, and her lovely young velvety delicate delta be tainted and torn—even then I

would go mad with tenderness at the mere sight of your dear
wan face, at the mere sound of your raucous young voice, my
Lolita.

In Humbert's most mannerist manner—hectic, writhing, self-falsifying,
self-caricaturing—this is still sincerity, and faced with this, the reader dare
not dissociate himself from Humbert in simple condemnation. With all we
now believe and feel about sexuality and self-responsibility, no one can call
Humbert's perversity a more significant moral fact than his ability to love.
And neither can the reader dissociate himself from the experience in simple
titillation or appreciation of the comedy and the fine writing. Nabokov has
taken the tradition of romantic fiction, and carried it forward into its next
stage; if Carmen, why not Lolita? Whatever answer we make, that is a
serious question, and Nabokov has put it to us seriously.

The moral theory I mean is an application of the doctrine of the immortality of art. Art can confer immortality, of a consciously limited and
conditional kind, by "singing" its subject, "celebrating" the experience it
describes, however painful or ignoble that may be. This is, however little,
the most that man can do to assert his values in the face of life's indifference,
and therefore art is glorious, in all its artificiality and trickery. The artist is a
kind of hero. Humbert killed Quilty because "One had to choose between
him and H. H., and one wanted H. H. to exist at least a couple of months
longer, so as to have him make you live in the minds of later generations."
And what Humbert wrote *is* the local and melancholy palliative of art, a
palliative to his misery, and a reparation to her memory, because it is an
immortalizing tribute to their experience. This describes and accounts for
the novel as a whole, texture and structure. It could be read by Lolita as his
tribute to her and to the events of their relationship. Its tone is true to their
tone to each other in the reported conversations and encounters. It does
confer upon her the immortality of art, and it is the kind of art—as distinct
from the kind of *Madame Bovary* or even *Anna Karenina*—which could be
felt as a tribute. And the melancholy and the inadequacy of the reparation
are fully acknowledged by—are a part of—the novel.

But *Lolita* was written by Nabokov, not by Humbert, and it is a tribute
to more than its heroine. The palliative Nabokov offers us is on a larger
scale, though of exactly the same kind, as what Humbert intended. It is an
intricately woven garland of mingled pain and delight, offered in tribute to
America. This is not only a matter of the overt hymning of the American
landscape, or the affectionate satire of the motels, the cars, the highways,
the curiosities. It is also a matter of characterization, and thematic characterization. Lolita herself is a part of America. She and her mother, their rela-

tions with each other and with their friends, the house and the town they live in are vividly American figures, in a vivid sketch of American life, the interest of which is quite independent of Humbert's personal drama. They are also thematically related to previous characterizations, those of Annabel and Valeria, in the way that America as a whole is related to Europe.

This relationship is a development toward realism, a mixed, part-painful, part-ignominious understanding of life, away from the romantic, the pastoral, the idyllic understanding associated with Europe. The idea of this development is made explicit in several places in which Lolita and Annabel are compared. It is *implicit* in the tawdry, comic, fake seaside scene in which Humbert first sees Lolita, compared with the real (but so much more simple and "romantic") seaside in which he knew Annabel. It is implicit again here:

> What drives me insane is the twofold nature of this nymphet—
> of every nymphet, perhaps; this mixture in my Lolita of tender
> dreamy childishness and a kind of eerie vulgarity, stemming
> from the snub-nosed cuteness of ads and magazine pictures,
> from the blurry pinkness of adolescent maidservants in the Old
> Country (smelling of crushed daisies and sweat); and from very
> young harlots disguised as children in provincial brothels; and
> then again, all this gets mixed up with the exquisite stainless
> tenderness seeping through the musk and the mud, through the
> dirt and the death, oh God, oh God.

He could not have said that about Annabel, and yet he needed to say it, for the full development of his complicated moral and aesthetic harmonies. Not only Lolita herself, but the Lolita experience, is "American," part beauty, part absurdity, part horror. That mixture of the dreamily childish with the eerily vulgar is what Humbert finds everywhere in America, and the substitution of that mixture for the idyllic simplicities of Europe is the major process of development for the novel. It is the condition of fulfilment of all Nabokov's potentialities as an artist.

The development from Valeria to Charlotte is primarily in substantiality:

> Had Charlotte been Valeria, I would have known how to handle
> the situation; and "handle" is the word I want. In the good old
> days, by merely twisting fat Valeria's brittle wrist (the one she
> had fallen upon from a bicycle) I could make her change her
> mind instantly; but anything of the sort in regard to Charlotte
> was unthinkable. Bland American Charlotte frightened me.

Charlotte is altogether a larger figure in the book, and Humbert is constantly brought up against reality in her. And in her case as in Lolita's, her substantiality is a matter of her Americanness. Annabel and Valeria are creatures of pastoral fantasy, in comparison; they fit completely into Humbert's dreams. Lolita and Charlotte continually upset, offend, elude, resist him and his dreams. They, and all America, are reality; though finding reality does not mean, for Nabokov, renouncing romance, but combining that with its opposite, in a stable counterpoint of the idyllic with the grotesque.

Indeed, Humbert himself stands in the same relation to his father as Lolita to Annabel, as Charlotte to Valeria, as America to Europe. His father's debonair and selfish sensuality was able to gratify itself all his life long in an atmosphere of universal admiration and fondness, general gaiety and wit, discriminating elegance and luxury. His father and two grandfathers had sold wine, jewels, and silk; Humbert's uncle sold perfumes; his English grandfathers had amusing, scholarly hobbies. Humbert was obviously destined to a similar career—to be a more intellectual version of his father—but life played the hideous trick of perversity upon him. The grotesque had to be interwoven with the idyllic. The beautiful Hotel Mirana was changed for a series of American motels. The point of the book is that the motels are more interesting, more vivid, more fully alive than the Mirana; that they, Lolita, America are embraced in full recognition of their differentness from Europe, their differentness from everything idyllic or even respectable, but in full enthusiastic appreciation. And since they represent more of life, as Nabokov sees life, it is life as a whole that is embraced. Thus the book is a tribute to America, and to human experience, in a way that expands without altering its function as a tribute to Lolita. And the immortality art can confer is thus a larger thing than the formula suggests, a thing closer to Lawrence's and Tolstoy's aims in art, since it is life itself that is immortalized.

I have already discussed the way in which the novel is "about" romantic love. Let me just say now that this theme is developed and resolved according to the pattern of the novel. That is, the major instance of love taken (the American instance, the Lolita instance) is very painful, ugly, unassimilable to romance; it is explicitly contrasted with the minor, perfect instance, and then described in insolent and brutal detail; but the total picture created is of a necessary interaction of very beautiful moments with very ugly ones. It is a development from idyllic romanticism to realistic romanticism, by means of interweaving the grotesque with the idealized in a convincing pattern.

It is only in this sense that I can understand Nabokov's sentence about aesthetic bliss. The novel gives us the sensation of being connected with other states of being where art is the norm; and art he either identifies with or groups with curiosity, tenderness, kindness, ecstasy. *Lolita* obviously creates moments for us in which curiosity, tenderness, ecstasy, beauty, art itself are radiantly realized, and it creates a world within which we can rely on such moments recurring. But, to justify a man in entering such a mental world, he needs to be sure that it is "realistic"—that it has taken adequate account of the ugliness of actual experience, and of the human impulse merely to make up such pretty dreams, merely to make itself see roses and hear violins. So *Lolita* must contain also moments of ugliness and pain as bitter and burning as any Nabokov could devise. And it must be infinitely skeptical about its own search for beauty, infinitely ironic about every mode of romanticism and idyll. Moreover, these anti-romantic modes of the imagination must be allowed to interpenetrate the romantic. Hence all the pornographic-seeming detail of the orgasm on the couch, so ugly and shocking as well as so brilliant and gay. Hence too all the trickery, all the warning against believing the narrator, against any unguarded response, throughout the novel. Only by giving full free play to both these anti-romantic tendencies, and by building a world that will contain them too, can the author justify those moments of perfect beauty and win for himself "aesthetic bliss."

This is the moral structure of *Lolita,* and it surely is strong enough to support and contain the anti-moral material the novel allows itself. A novel is not pornographic (except in the sense that it can be used as pornography) when its interest in sexual excitement is a necessary part of such large and serious interests. It is not anti-cultural when its cynicism (Humbert's cynicism) dramatizes an alienation which is so movingly, though unobtrusively, placed and judged.

But none of this contradicts Tolstoy's assumed condemnation of the novel. All we have been saying is true only from a point of view completely sympathetic with the author, a view taken from a point, so to speak, inside the novel. This is the perfect reading of the novel, and novels do not exist only in that form. Culturally speaking, they exist much more in the form of imperfect readings—as understood from outside the novel, in very imperfect sympathy with the author's intentions. *Lolita* can be used as pornography; in fact it will be, and almost must be, and by highly trained readers as well as by the untrained. It will also have, in its measure, an anti-cultural effect of weakening taboos and fostering cynicism. There is something powerfully disintegrative in Nabokov's sensibility, and, though the novel's form contains and transmutes that something, the total effect of reading it— even on highly trained readers—is not likely to be controlled by the form. *Lolita is* in fact the product and the agent of a corrupt culture.

If then we, like Tolstoy, were ready to judge art primarily by cultural criteria, we could, and would have to, condemn *Lolita*. Tolstoy followed Plato, and said better no art than bad art, which means better aesthetically bad art than morally bad. But we, presumably, are committed to using primarily aesthetic criteria, and to preferring aesthetically good art. We are committed to judging a novel primarily on its perfect reading, seeing it in perfect sympathy with the author's intentions, understanding it from inside; however rare, in cultural fact, such a reading may be; however little that reading may coincide with the book's effective meaning; however "exclusive," to use Tolstoy's term, the audience for that version of the book.

This obligation on the critic is a necessary correlative of the freedom of the artist, and we of the liberal tradition are presumably committed to that freedom. Nabokov is a fine example of the free artist, and a fine symbol of what we are committed to. He is free first in the sense of refusing all allegiance to nonaesthetic schemes of value, and aggressively, positively refusing, as well as negatively; he affronts and injures those schemes of value; he is not only nonideological, he is anti-ideological. And this freedom he so fully takes necessitates the other freedom we were discussing— his claim, his right, to be judged only from inside the special world he has created. His justification of those freedoms, and what they cost us in affronts and injuries to our personal and collective sensibilities, is the novel itself. Given its perfect reading, *Lolita* is a brilliant and beautiful experience, satisfying our most purely moral sense as well as all the others. What is there in Tolstoy's "art of the future," Soviet literature, that can compare with it? But that comparison is not the point. It is the contrast, within our own case, between what we gain and what we lose, by our effective philosophy of art, which seems to me so interesting.

*L*olita: The Springboard of Parody

Alfred Appel, Jr.

Nabokov regards with profound skepticism the possibilities of autobiographical revelation. When Fyodor shaves himself in *The Gift*, "A pale self-portrait looked out of the mirror with the serious eyes of all self-portraits"; Nabokov does not abide such portraits. "Manifold self-awareness" is not to be achieved through solemn introspection, certainly not through the diarist's compulsive egotism, candid but totally self-conscious self-analysis, carefully created "honesty," willful irony, and studied self-deprecation. Nabokov burlesqued the literary diary as far back as 1934. Near the end of *Despair*, Hermann's first-person narrative "degenerates into a diary"—"the lowest form of literature"—and this early parody is fully realized in *Lolita*, especially in chapter eleven, part one, when Humbert incorporates into his narrative a diary "destroyed" five years before. His entire prison "journal" seems to be written before our eyes. "I notice the slip of my pen in the preceding paragraph, but please do not correct it, Clarence" [his lawyer and caretaker of the manuscript], Humbert remarks. Several other "mistakes" are left intact, thus creating the illusion that Humbert's manuscript is a first draft, unaltered, written in great haste but with passion, and the hapless literal-minded reader may embrace it as the most "sincere" form of self-portraiture possible. But of course all the worst propensities of the diarist are embodied in Humbert's rhetoric, parodying the first-person singular's almost inevitable solipsism and most tendentious assumptions about self, and the reader who is late in realizing this has had his own assumptions parodied.

From *Nabokov: The Man and His Work*, edited by L. S. Dembo. © 1967 by the Regents of the University of Wisconsin. The University of Wisconsin Press, 1967.

Nabokov has rejected a romantic or transcendental notion of self; another of Humbert's jocose but significant appellations is Jean-Jacques Humbert. The unified, definitive self is a joke to Nabokov, for the infinite possibilities of its development are circumscribed by the warped mirror in which we perceive ourselves and the world. Unlike those modern writers who continually bemoan the loss of the self in the modern world, Nabokov accepts the fragmentation, and within the terrifying limitations he coolly acknowledges, Nabokov lets Humbert define himself however he must, and fulfill his human condition, albeit obsessional and aberrant. The reader who can follow the process of involution and calmly play the games effected by parody, and realize their implications, will not worry whether Nabokov "approves" or "disapproves" of his characters.

What is extraordinary about *Lolita* is not the presence or absence of the author's "moral position," but the way in which Nabokov enlists us, against our will, on Humbert's side. "Pity is the password," says John Shade, speaking for his creator. Nabokov purposely takes a shocking subject in *Lolita,* and when we are sympathetic to Humbert, Nabokov has successfully expanded our potential for compassion, and has demonstrated that the certainty of our moral feelings is far more tenuous than we ever care to admit. We know exactly what Nabokov means about the contest between the author and the reader when we almost find ourselves wishing Humbert well during his agonizing first night with Lolita at The Enchanted Hunters, or appreciating Humbert's situation when the drugged Lolita occupies an "unfair amount of pillow." "Mesmer Mesmer" is one of the pseudonyms Humbert considered but rejected. It would be a fitting cognomen, given the power and effect of his rhetoric, since Humbert has figuratively made the reader his accomplice in both statutory rape and murder. Needless to say, the rhetoric of morality can be just as manipulative, and what is worse, it may not connect meaningfully with emotion of any kind. Because Lolita seduces Humbert she might seem to be the agent of immorality, but the irony is another trap in the game: this is just the kind of easy release from culpability which we are too ready to accept; it does not mitigate the existence of their ensuing two years together, nor the fact that Humbert has denied Lolita her youth, whatever its qualities may be. It should be clear that when Nabokov says that there is "No moral in tow" in *Lolita,* he is not denying it any moral resonance, but simply asserting that his intentions are not didactic.

Lolita is a moral novel in the fullest sense. Humbert is both victimizer and victim, culprit and judge. Throughout the narrative he is literally and figuratively pursued by his double, Clare Quilty, who is by turns ludicrous and absurd, sinister and grotesque. Prior to his full-dress appearance in chapter thirty-five, part two, when he is killed by Humbert, Quilty is seen or alluded to more than fifty times, not including the several references to Aubrey McFate (as Hum "dub[s] that devil of mine"). Although Quilty is usually not mentioned by name, direct clues are planted through allusions to his uncle, Dr. Ivor Quilty, who is the Hazes' neighbor and dentist, and in Humbert's mention of *Who's Who in the Limelight,* which includes an entry under "Quilty, Clare, American dramatist," where he is listed as the author of *Fatherly Love* and *The Little Nymph.* For a while Humbert is certain that his "shadow" and nemesis is his Swiss cousin, Detective Trapp, and when Lolita agrees and says, "Perhaps he is Trapp," she is summarizing Quilty's role in the novel. So complete is the respective entrapment of both Humbert and the reader that hardly ten or fifteen pages can go by in the course of part one without Quilty's fleeting presence, and in part two he becomes omnipresent, for even after killing him, Humbert still feels "all covered with Quilty." The creator of "private movies" of Sade's *Justine* is always in the wings, so to speak, because he formulates Humbert's sense of guilt and the reader's prurient curiosity, and his name lends itself to obvious but significant wordplay: Clare Quilty is clearly guilty.

Humbert knows he is clearly guilty, though he goes about saying it in oblique and unexpected ways. As his narrative draws to a close, Humbert's stance becomes increasingly "moral," but readers must be wary of the most overtly confessional passages, such as Humbert's recreation of the crucial scene in which, after a three-year search, he confronts a pregnant ex-nymphet and, in a long passage which should not be excised, realizes that as "clearly as I know I am to die, that I loved her more than anything I had ever seen or imagined on earth," in spite of her "ruined looks and her adult, rope-veined narrow hands and her goose-flesh white arms." It would be an understatement to say that the tone of the entire passage is ambiguous: the baby's dream, the injunction to an imaginary judge and jury, the interpolations in French, the parodic echo of Billy Graham's exhortation ("Make those twenty-five steps. Now."), and the purposeful banality of Humbert's promise ("And we shall live happily ever after") almost annihilate Humbert's declaration of love, but not quite. Miraculously enough, one believes in his love, not because of any confession, but in spite of it. "I had always thought that wringing one's hands was a fictional gesture," Humbert says, and the comic turns are a protection against such rhetorical gestures and serve to isolate, if only for a moment, the arresting image of a wan and helpless girl.

Humbert's fullest expressions of "grief" are qualified, if not undercut completely, and these passages represent a series of traps in which Nabokov again parodies the reader's expectations by having Humbert say what the reader wants to hear. "I was a pentapod monster, but I loved you. I was despicable and brutal, and turpid, and everything"; it is easy to confess, but the moral vocabulary we employ so readily may go no deeper than Humbert's parody of it. Although Humbert "quote[s] an old poet," "The moral sense in mortals is the duty/ We have to pay on mortal sense of beauty," one may wonder if he does indeed pay any duty. The payment is in fact exacted throughout the narrative, and is in part expressed in the grotesque gyrations of Humbert's tone: "Ah, gentle drivers gliding through summer's black nights, what frolics, what twists of lust, you might see from your impeccable highways if Kumfy Kabins were suddenly drained of their pigments and became as transparent as boxes of glass." Gentle readers gliding through Humbert's prose are similarly subjected to jolting twists of tone—a rhetorical trapdoor that opens with absurd suddenness, an unexpected downhill slide, a lyrical or humorous lift that momentarily relaxes the tension, then, without warning, another trapdoor. Such passages are free of any transitional phrases that might allow a logical and gradual shift in tone; the effect can be chilling. "She was very tall," Humbert says of Jean Farlow, "wore either slacks with sandals or billowing skirts with ballet slippers, drank any strong liquor in any amount, had had two miscarriages, wrote stories about animals, painted, as the reader knows, landscapes, was already nursing the cancer that was to kill her at thirty-three, and was hopelessly unattractive to me." The sudden oscillations between the horrific and the humorous catch our laughter short, creating a tension that Humbert's jollity can never quite release; what Nabokov has called Humbert's "rhetorical venom" is turned back upon the narrator, affording an implicit commentary on his own acts.

"We continued our grotesque journey," Humbert says at one point, and the summary adjective is well-chosen, for the ultimate morality of *Lolita* is expressed through the grotesque. Those who are uneasy with Nabokov the *immoraliste* may find necessary solace in the carefully manipulated changes on the grotesque which proliferate in *Lolita*. Humbert's self-disgust and loathing and guilt are projected into almost all the so-called human beings Humbert "sees" or, more accurately, reports having seen: Quilty; Gaston Godin; Miss Opposite, the crippled neighbor; random carhops, bellboys, and parking-lot attendants; the room clerk, Mr. Swine; the old barber in Kasbeam; and Dick Schiller, Lolita's almost deaf husband, who is assisted by a one-armed young man named Bill, of whom Humbert comments, "It was then noticed that one of the few thumbs remaining to

Bill was bleeding (not such a wonder-worker at all)." The grotesque is meaningfully present in the most casual of encounters, as when Frank, a motel attendant, stands in the doorway, his hand on its jamb:

> At twenty paces Frank used to look a mountain of health; at five, as now, he was a ruddy mosaic of scars—had been blown through a wall overseas; but despite nameless injuries he was able to man a tremendous truck, fish, hunt, drink, and buoy-antly dally with roadside ladies. That day, either because it was such a great holiday, or simply because he wanted to divert a sick man, he had taken off the glove he usually wore on his left hand (the one pressing against the side of the door) and revealed to the fascinated sufferer not only an entire lack of fourth and fifth fingers, but also a naked girl, with cinnabar nipples and indigo delta, charmingly tattooed on the back of his crippled hand, its index and middle digit making her legs while his wrist bore her flower-crowned head. Oh, delicious . . . reclining against the woodwork, like some sly fairy.

As Humbert quietly says to Lolita when they notice the fragmented and surreal limbs of a department store mannikin, "Look well. Is not that a good symbol of something or other?" But this potential booby trap is only a dud, for it *is* a good symbol, in a refreshingly direct way, and Humbert is only dissembling, though symbol-mongering critics may accept the warning. The entire physical world of *Lolita* seems to be maimed, and the animate and inanimate share each other's properties in startling and unsettling ways. The car which runs over Charlotte Haze has doors "open like wings," and the driver's old father lies on the lawn in a faint, "like a death-size wax figure," an "old man-doll," whom a nurse "watered on the green bank where he lay." Even Humbert's car limps. The hunchbacks, the tennis-playing "Boschian cripples," the broken nose of a man wiping down Hum's windshield, Humbert's terrifying dream of Lolita, his self-styled animal characteristics of ape, spider, and octopus—the possible parodic allusions to Poe, Dostoyevski, and Stevenson notwithstanding—and the numerous other seemingly gratuitous grotesque details are all metaphoric for the horror implicit in Humbert's life, for his suffering, his sense of shame and guilt and self-hate. "And I have still other smothered memories," says Humbert towards the end of *Lolita*, "now unfolding themselves into limbless monsters of pain."

Thus Nabokov uses the grotesque to express the anguish behind Humbert's rhetoric, the pain at the center of his playfulness, the price he must pay for having loved the way he was fated to love; one should not forget that Humbert dies of a coronary shortly after finishing his "book." Because he knows that he has treated Lolita like a thing, Humbert's world seems to have been reduced to monstrous "thinghood," and his grotesque projections are by way of his "confession": " 'Did you happen to see—' [Lolita] I asked of a hunchback sweeping the floor . . . He had, the old lecherer." Although the mask has not been removed, it has been penetrated, for the "slipperyself" 's moral judgments on its "public" acts have been transposed to the scene—inscape as landscape—and Nabokov is sly enough to have Humbert say something almost to that effect: "I am afraid, Clarence . . . I did not keep any notes, and have at my disposal only an atrociously crippled tour book in three volumes, almost a symbol of my torn and tattered past." Nabokov has parodied all "literary" confessions that would offer a strident and rhetorical expression of egotism as a revelation of the soul, and at the same time has succeeded in suggesting the deepest reaches of that soul. In their own way, Humbert's "tragic notes" are indeed from underground, but only because they embody both the "truth and a caricature of it."

This hazardous equipoise is also sustained in the doubling of Quilty and Humbert, for Quilty is at once a projection of Humbert's guilt and a parody of the psychological double. The double motif figures prominently throughout Nabokov, from the early thirties in *Despair* and *Laughter in the Dark* (where the Albinus-Axel Rex pairing rehearses the Humbert-Quilty doubling), to *Sebastian Knight* and on through *Bend Sinister,* the story "Scenes from the Life of a Double Monster," *Lolita, Pnin,* and *Pale Fire,* which offers a monumental doubling (or, more properly, tripling). It is probably the most intricate and profound of all doppelgänger novels, written at precisely the time when it seemed that the double theme had been exhausted in modern literature, and this achievement was very likely made possible by Nabokov's elaborate parody of the theme in *Lolita,* which renewed his sense of the artistic efficacy of another literary "thing which had once been fresh and bright but which was now worn to a thread."

By making Quilty *too* clearly guilty, Nabokov is assaulting the convention of the good and evil "dual selves" found in the traditional double tale. Humbert would let some of us believe that when he kills Quilty in chapter thirty-five, part two, the good poet has exorcised the bad monster, but the two are finally not to be clearly distinguished: when Humbert and Quilty wrestle, "I rolled over him. We rolled over me. They rolled over him. We rolled over us." Although the parody culminates in this "silent, soft, formless tussle on the part of two literati," it is sustained throughout the novel. In the traditional doppelgänger fiction the double representing the reprehensible self is often described as an ape. In *The Possessed,* Stavrogin tells Verkhovensky, "you're my ape"; in *Dr. Jekyll and Mr. Hyde,* Hyde plays "apelike tricks," attacks and kills with "apelike fury" and "apelike spite"; and in Poe's "The Murders in the Rue Morgue," the criminal self is literally an ape. But "good" Humbert undermines the doubling by often calling himself an ape, rather than Quilty, and when the two face one another, Quilty also calls Humbert an ape. This transference is forcefully underscored when Humbert refers to himself as running along like "Mr. Hyde," his "talons still tingling." In Conrad's *Heart of Darkness,* Kurtz is Marlow's "shadow" and "shade." Although Humbert calls Quilty his "shadow," the pun on Humbert's name suggests that he is as much a shadow as Quilty, and like the shadow self in Andersen's tale, Humbert is dressed all in black. Quilty in fact first regards Humbert as possibly being "some familiar and innocuous hallucination" of his own, and in the novel's closing moments the masked narrator addresses Lolita and completes this transferral: "And do not pity C. Q. One had to choose between him and H. H., and one wanted H. H. to exist at least a couple of months longer, so as to have him make you live in the minds of later generations." The book might have been told by "C. Q.," the doubling reversed; "H. H." is simply a better artist, more likely to possess the "secret of durable pigments."

If the Humbert-Quilty doubling is a conscious parody of "William Wilson," it is with good reason, for Poe's story is unusual among doppelgänger tales in that it presents a reversal of the conventional situation: the weak and evil self is the main character, pursued by the moral self, whom he kills. Nabokov goes further and with one vertiginous sweep stands the convention on its head: in terms of the nineteenth-century double tale, it should not even be necessary to kill Quilty and what he represents, for Humbert has already declared his love for Lolita *before* he goes to Quilty's Pavor Manor, and in asking the no longer nymphic Lolita to go away with him, he has transcended his obsession. As a "symbolic" act, the killing is gratuitous; the parodic design is complete.

Quilty rightly balks at his symbolic role: "I'm not responsible for the rapes of others. Absurd!" he tells Humbert, and his words are well taken, for in this scene Humbert *is* trying to make him totally responsible, and the poem which he has Quilty read aloud reinforces his effort, and again demonstrates how a Nabokov parody moves beyond the "obscure fun" of stylistic imitation to connect with the most serious region of the book. It begins as a parody of Eliot's *Ash-Wednesday* but ends by undercutting all the confessing in which "remorseful" Humbert has just been engaged: "because of all you did/because of all I did not/ you have to die." Since Quilty has been described as "the American Maeterlinck," it goes without saying that his ensuing death scene should be extravagantly "symbolic." Because one is not easily rid of an "evil" self, Quilty is almost impossible to kill, but the idea of exorcism is rendered absurd by his comically prolonged death throes, which, in the spirit of canto 5 of *The Rape of the Lock,* burlesque the gore and rhetoric of literary death scenes ranging from the Elizabethan drama to the worst of detective novels. Quilty returns to the scene of the crime—a bed—and it is here that Humbert finally corners him. When Humbert fires his remaining bullets at close range, Quilty "lay back, and a big pink bubble with juvenile connotations formed on his lips, grew to the size of a toy balloon, and vanished." The last details emphasize the mock-symbolic association with Lolita; the monstrous self that has devoured Lolita, bubblegum, childhood and all, is "symbolically" dead, but as the bubble explodes, so does the Gothic doppelgänger convention, with all its own "juvenile connotations" about identity, and we learn shortly that Humbert is still "all covered with Quilty." Guilt is not to be exorcised so readily—McFate is McFate, to coin a Humbertism—and the ambiguities of human experience and identity are not to be reduced to mere "dualities." Instead of the successful integration of a neatly divisible self, we are left with "Clare Obscure" and "quilted Quilty," the patchwork self. Quilty refuses to die, just as the recaptured nose, in Gogol's extraordinary double story of that name, would not at first stick to its owner's face. The reader who has expected the solemn moral-ethical absolutes of a Poe, Dostoyevski, Mann, or Conrad doppelgänger fiction instead discovers himself adrift in a fantastic, comic cosmos more akin to Gogol's. Having hoped that Humbert would master his "secret sharer," we find rather that his quest for his "slippery self" figuratively resembles Major Kovaliov's frantic chase after his own nose through the spectral streets of St. Petersburg, and that Humbert's "quest" has its mock "ending" in a final confrontation that, like the end of *The Overcoat,* is not a confrontation at all.

The parodic references to R. L. Stevenson suggest that Nabokov had in mind Henry Jekyll's painfully earnest discovery of the "truth" that "man is not only one, but truly two. I say two, because the state of my own knowledge does not pass beyond that point. Others will follow, others will outstrip me on the same lines." The "serial selves" of *Pale Fire* "outstrip" Stevenson and a good many other writers, and rather than undermining Humbert's guilt, the double parody in *Lolita* locks Humbert within that prison of mirrors in which the "real self" and its masks blend into one another, the refracted outlines of good and evil becoming terrifyingly confused.

Humbert's search for the whereabouts and identity of Detective Trapp (Quilty) invites the reader to wend his way through a labyrinth of clues in order to solve this mystery, a process which parodies the Poe "tale of ratiocination." When Humbert finds Lolita and presses her for her abductor's name,

> She said really it was useless, she would never tell, but on the other hand, after all—"Do you really want to know who it was? Well it was—"
> And softly, confidentially, arching her thin eyebrows and puckering her parched lips, she emitted, a little mockingly, somewhat fastidiously, not untenderly, in a kind of muted whistle, the name that the astute reader has guessed long ago.
> Waterproof. Why did a flash from Hourglass Lake cross my consciousness? I, too, had known it, without knowing it, all along. There was no shock, no surprise. Quietly the fusion took place, and everything fell into order, into the pattern of branches that I have worn throughout this memoir with the express purpose of having the ripe fruit fall at the right moment; yes, with the express and perverse purpose of rendering—she was talking but I sat melting in my golden peace—of rendering that golden and monstrous peace through the satisfaction of logical recognition, which my most inimical reader should experience now.

Even here Humbert withholds Quilty's identity, though the "astute reader" may recognize that "Waterproof" is a clue which leads back to an early scene at the lake, in which Charlotte had said that Humbert's watch was waterproof and Jean Farlow had alluded to Quilty's Uncle Ivor (by his first name only), and then had almost mentioned Clare Quilty by name: Ivor "told me a completely indecent story about his nephew. It appears—" but she is interrupted and the chapter ends. This teasing exercise in ratiocination—"peace" indeed!—is the detective trap—another parody of the reader's assumptions and expectations, as though even the most astute reader could ever fully discover the identity of Quilty, Humbert, or of himself.

Provided with Quilty's name, Humbert now makes his way to Pavor Manor, that latter-day House of Usher, where the extended and variegated parodies of Poe are laid to rest. All the novel's parodic themes are concluded in this chapter. Its importance is telescoped by Humbert's conclusion that "This, I said to myself, was the end of the ingenious play staged for me by Quilty." In form, of course, this bravura set piece is not a play, but as a summary parodic commentary on the main action, it does function in the manner of an Elizabethan play-within-the-play, and its "staging" under-scores once more the game element central to the book.

When indestructible Quilty dies, he fittingly subsides "in a purple heap," the color of his prose and of a good many of Humbert's quilted verbal patterns. Quilty's "genre, his type of humor," says Humbert, "had affinities with my own. He mimed and mocked me." Quilty's penchant for "log-adaedaly and logomancy" double Humbert's own excesses, and Quilty's death scene rhetoric and trail of recondite, "insulting pseudonyms," duly commented on by Humbert ("obvious"; "trite poke"; "in horrible taste"; "silly but funny"; "shoddy") represent Humbert's act of self-criticism, and ultimately Nabokov's, too. "His main trait was his passion for tantalization. Goodness, what a tease the poor fellow was! He challenged my scholarship." Humbert's "cryptogrammic paper chase" after Quilty is Nabokov's self-parody of the involuted butterfly pattern running through the book's sub-stratum and a compressed parody of the author-reader conflict sustained over the course of the trap-laden book (Quilty "succeeded in thoroughly enmesh-ing me . . . in his demoniacal game"; "touché, reader!" says Humbert, gran-ting us a point in the game while mocking our delight in recognizing one of Quilty's most obvious literary jokes). Nabokov's own proclivities are re-flected in Humbert's puns, which are in turn refracted in Quilty's worse puns. A double self-parody spirals in upon Quilty, who seals his own fate in the eyes of both the narrator and the author when he tells Humbert, "you know, as the Bard said, with that cold in his head, to borrow and to borrow and to borrow," and for that, Quilty deserves to die.

Nabokov has written thirteen books in Russian and ten in English (not including his translations). In the afterword to *Lolita,* he corrects the critic who thought that *Lolita* was "the record of my love affair with the romantic novel," and suggests that "The substitution 'English language' for 'roman-tic novel' would make this elegant formula more correct." But *Lolita* doesn't chronicle the happiest "love affair," and "the second-rate brand of English" [sic] which Nabokov says he has adopted in place of his "untram-meled" and "rich" Russian idiom is belied by the eloquent and elegant English prose of *Speak, Memory,* the book previous to *Lolita.* This suggests that the language of *Lolita*—which might be termed colloquial baroque—is both a conscious parody of all efforts to acquire a "fine style" (including *Speak, Memory*) and a parodic record of the painful struggle to capture in any language the essence of what Albinus, in *Laughter in the Dark,* calls "a thing quite impossible to capture," whether it be the past, as in *Speak, Memory,* or the grace and beauty of a nymphet. "What a tale might be told," imagines Albinus, "the tale of an artist's vision, the happy journey of eye and brush," and Nabokov tells it in *Lolita,* but it is a journey through "black Humberland." By purposely making his narrator a decidedly second-rate man of letters—a *"manqué* talent"—Nabokov can not only show us the struggle more clearly, but may incorporate into Humbert's caprices a network of literary jokes and minor parodies which express concrete and consistent ideas concerning language, literature, and the limitations inherent in just such an effort as Humbert's.

Nabokov has said that poetry is the "mystery of the irrational perceived through rational words." Throughout his work he confronts the central problem of postromantic art and literature and, using parody and self-parody as "springboards," offers a critique of romanticism. At its very best, Nabokov's verbal slapstick will thus suggest the inner tensions which threaten to break down a character and with him the language, especially when he is trying to communicate that "mystery," to re-create an abyss. Cincinnatus in *Invitation to a Beheading* tells Millie, his twelve-year old inamorata, "I'm exhausted—I didn't weep a slink last night," just as two decades later, in their "seduction" scene at The Enchanted Hunters, Humbert says to Lolita,

> "What's the katter with misses?" I muttered (word-control gone) into her hair.
> "If you must know," she said, "you do it the wrong way."
> "Show, wight ray."
> "All in good time," responded the spoonerette.

> *Seva ascendes, pulsata, brulans, kitzelans, dementissima. Elevator clatterans, pausa, clatterans, populus in corridoro. Hanc nisi mors mihi adimet nemo! Juncea puellula, jo pensavo fondissime, nobserva nihil quidquam . . .*

The language of Horace and Catullus (both of whom are mentioned in *Lolita*) is appropriate to this modern, if hysterical, elegiast—the rush of "Latin" registering background noises and Humbert's panic and garbled expression of undying love. At moments of extreme crisis, Humbert croaks incomprehensibly, losing more than his expropriated English, for his attempts "to fix once for all the perilous magic of nymphets" almost resist language altogether, carrying him close to the edge of nonlanguage and a figurative silence. Thus Humbert significantly announces the scene as a "Parody of silence," and far from being nonsensical, the ensuing nonsense Latin is a parodic stream of consciousness, affording a brief critical comment on a technique which Nabokov finds unsatisfactory, even in the novels of Joyce, whom he reveres. "We think not in words but in shadows of words," Nabokov has said, "James Joyce's mistake in those otherwise marvelous mental soliloquies of his consists in that he gives too much verbal body to words." To Nabokov, the unconnected impressions and associations that impinge on the mind are irrational until they are consciously ordered; and to order them in art is to fulfill a virtually moral obligation, for without rational language, man has "grown a very/ landfish, languageless,/ a monster," as Thersites says of Ajax in Shakespeare's *Troilus and Cressida.* Nabokov and his beleaguered first person narrators have looked into the void, but they do not reproduce it; the "private language" of Zemblan in *Pale Fire* is the nearest Nabokov has come, and its efficacy is totally rejected through parody. In contrast to the state of "silence" towards which so much recent art variously evolves or aspires—whether Samuel Beckett, William Burroughs, John Cage, or Ad Reinhardt—Nabokov's deeply humanistic art reaffirms the reality and majesty of language. Even the imprisoned and doomed Cincinnatus is "already thinking of how to set up an alphabet" which might humanize his dystopian world.

Humbert says of his artistic labors, "The beastly and beautiful merged at one point, and it is that borderline I would like to fix, and I feel I fail to do so utterly. Why?" The rhetorical question is coy enough because he answered it at the beginning of his narrative; he hasn't failed, but neither can he ever be entirely successful, because "Oh, my Lolita, I have only words to play with!"—an admission many postromantic writers would not make. Nabokov's remark about Joyce giving "too much verbal body to words" succinctly defines the burden the symbolists placed on the word, as though it were an endlessly resonant object rather than one component in a referential system of signs. As G. D. Josipovici observes, "To try and use them as objects is . . . to repeat the mistake Humbert made with Lolita: to try and possess carnally what can only be possessed imaginatively." Nabokov's novels are filled with allusions to other writers, but never more meaningfully than in *Lolita,* since Humbert's acknowledgment of the limitations of language leaves so many writers open to criticism, especially the romantic poets. "Are you troubled by Romantic Associations?" Charlotte inquires of her new husband, and Keats, Byron, and Blake are humorously invoked. Humbert calls Lolita a "fair daemon child," which makes her a kind of Belle Dame Sans Merci in bobby sox. But the main recipient of Nabokov's parody of romanticism is Edgar Poe.

Like Poe's first-person narrators who incorporate poems into their tales ("The Assignation," "Ligeia," "The Fall of the House of Usher"), Humbert interpolates liberal amounts of his own verse, and its comically blatant rhymes suggest an overly zealous application of Poe's ideas on rhyme in "The Poetic Principle." Nabokov's choice of both subject matter and narrator parody Poe's designation, in "The Philosophy of Composition," of the "most poetical topic in the world": "the death of a beautiful woman . . . and equally is it beyond doubt that the lips best suited for such topic are those of a bereaved lover." Both Annabel Lee and Lolita "die," the latter in terms of her fading nymphic qualities and escape from Humbert, who invokes yet another of Poe's lost ladies when he calls Lolita "Lenore" (the subject of "Lenore" and "The Raven"), a reference which also points to "The Philosophy of Composition," since that essay concerns "The Raven."

The speaker in Poe's "Lenore" gropes for the right elegiac chord: "How *shall* the ritual, then, be read?—the requiem how be sung/ By you—by yours, the evil eye,—by yours, the slanderous tongue/ That did to death the innocence that died, and died so young?" How shall it be "sung" is also the main question in *Lolita,* and Nabokov found his answer in a parodic style that seems to parody *all* styles, including its own. This self-parodying tone is well-defined by a writer much admired by Nabokov. Jorge Luis Borges says that "the Baroque is that style which deliberately exhausts (or tries to exhaust) its possibilities and borders on its own caricature." "You talk like a book, *Dad,*" Lolita tells Humbert; and in order to protect his own efforts to capture her essence, he tries to exhaust the "fictional gestures," such as Edgar Poe's, which would reduce the nymphet's ineffable qualities to a convention of language or literature. "Only in the tritest of terms," says Humbert, "can I describe Lo's features: I might say her hair is auburn, and her lips are red as licked red candy, the lower one prettily plump—oh, that I were a lady writer who could have her pose naked in a naked light!" "Well-read Humbert" will imitate the locution of a famous writer, try it on for size—"We came to know—*nous connûmes,* to use a Flaubertian intonation"—toy with it—"*Nous connûmes* (this is a royal fun)"—and then abandon it for something else. More than fifty writers are treated in this spirit, ranging from Dante and Petrarch to Molnar and Maeterlinck, as though only through parody and caricature can Humbert prevent the possibility that his "memoir" might finally be nothing more than what the authorial voice in *Invitation to a Beheading* asks of its captive creation: "Or is this all but obsolete romantic rot, Cincinnatus?"

That *Lolita* is not in any way "obsolete" results from Nabokov's realization of the ultimate implications of Proust's injunction to writers "to indulge in the cleansing, exorcising pastime of parody." Because Nabokov's use of parody is like Sebastian Knight's—"a clown developing wings, an angel mimicking a tumbler pigeon"—he is able to have it both ways.

Humbert's baroque language constitutes a virtuoso balancing or juggling act, for there are intervals when Humbert does capture Lolita's "essential grace," moments when, in the midst of the cascading puns and parodies, one has a glimpse of the "borderline [where] the beastly and beautiful merged," as in the scene where she plays tennis. It is a crucial necessity to recognize the tonal oscillations between his "beastly" and "beautiful" intonations, and to understand that one enables Humbert to realize the other. At the conclusion of Humbert's extended description of Lolita's tennis game, which occurs shortly before she is "kidnapped," the butterfly rises from its confines in the hermetic substructure of the novel, and in a single-line paragraph that it has to itself, flutters across the page: "An inquisitive butterfly passed, dipping, between us."

Its appearance foreshadows the transcendent moment of felicity which has carried Humbert beyond the frightening solipsism of his lust and has enabled him to write his narrative. At the end of the novel, after crazily driving on the wrong, "mirror" side of the highway, Humbert turns off the road and rides up a grassy slope, coming to a "gentle, rocking stop." Immobile, suspended in felicity, he experiences "A kind of thoughtful Hegelian synthesis linking up two dead women," a realization of Quilty's play-within-the-novel, *The Enchanted Hunters,* which featured Lolita as a bewitching "farmer's daughter who imagines herself to be a woodland witch, or Diana," and seven hunters, six of them "red-capped, uniformly attired." A "last-minute kiss was to enforce the play's profound message, namely, that mirage and reality merge in love." When Humbert asks a pregnant and veiny-armed Lolita to go away with him, he demonstrates that the mirage of the past (the nymphic Lolita as his lost "Annabel") and the reality of the present (the Charlotte-like woman Lolita is becoming) *have* merged in love, a "synthesis linking up two dead women."

The play's "message" also describes the "aesthetic bliss" of artistic creation, and one involuted turn in the "plot" of *The Enchanted Hunters* almost reveals the hand of an enchanted hunter named Nabokov: "a seventh Hunter (in a green cap, the fool) was a Young Poet, and he insisted, much to Diana's annoyance, that she and the entertainment provided (dancing nymphs, and elves, and monsters) were his, the Poet's invention." Humbert is Nabokov's creation just as Lolita is Humbert's, and for a summary comment, one looks to the narrator of *The Real Life of Sebastian Knight,* who, in speaking of *The Prismatic Bezel,* has preempted Nabokov's critics by limpidly presaging the entire parodic design and progression of *Lolita:*

> I have tried my best to show the workings of the book, at least
> some of its workings. Its charm, humour and pathos can only be

appreciated by direct reading. But for enlightenment of those who felt baffled by its habit of metamorphosis, or merely disgusted at finding something incompatible with the idea of a "nice book" in the discovery of a book's being an utterly new one, I should like to point out that *The Prismatic Bezel* can be thoroughly enjoyed once it is understood that the heroes of the book are what can be loosely called "methods of composition." It is as if a painter said: look, here I'm going to show you not the painting of a landscape, but the painting of different ways of painting a certain landscape, and I trust their harmonious fusion will disclose the landscape as I intend you to see it.

The lepidopteral game is but one of several reminders that *Lolita* is to Nabokov a deeply personal book. Like many of his characters, Humbert is an émigré, and Nabokov has been an exile for his entire adult life. It is a fact which characterizes a state of mind and spirit. Since leaving Russia in 1919 he has never owned a house and even today resides in a hotel. But the theme of exile in Nabokov's work is not merely a matter of the special circumstances of his life, for the figure of the exile embodies the human condition in our time, and no one has written more movingly about this figure than Nabokov. But the exile has his past—like the movie extras in "The Assistant Producer," that may well be all that he does have—and in *Speak, Memory,* Nabokov recreates the past, making it as vivid as the present. But the obsessive nostalgia that is so central to Nabokov's vision is ultimately no substitute for a viable life in the present, and among other things, *Lolita* is a devastating self-criticism of the reflexive attempt to move out of time, a self-parody of the psychological pastoral, and as such, it is Nabokov's own answer to his previous book, *Speak, Memory.* As Humbert says, near the end of the novel, "I was weeping again, drunk on the impossible past." Even Lolita tells him that "the past was the past," and his efforts to recapture it are made more than ludicrous by the congruent parody of Poe and psychiatry. If we envision Lolita and the brief time span of her nymphic years as a correlative for the past, we see how irrevocably self-destructive it is to live in that impossible past. "She had entered my world," says Humbert, "umber and black Humberland"—the shadowland of memory, a punning world where one shadow pursues another, and is destroyed in the process (see above).

As an exile, Nabokov of course had to write *Lolita* in English. "My private tragedy, which cannot, and indeed should not, be anybody's con-

cern," he says, "is that I had to abandon my natural idiom." But his "private tragedy" is our concern, for in varying degrees it involves us all. Nabokov's search for the language adequate to *Lolita* is Humbert's search for the language that will reach Lolita, and it is a representative search, a heightened emblem of all of our attempts to communicate. "A penny for your thoughts, I said, and she stretched out her palm at once." It is the almost insuperable distance between those thoughts and that palm which Nabokov has measured so accurately and so movingly in *Lolita:* the distance between people, the distance separating love from lovemaking, mirage from reality—the desperate extent of all human need and desire. "I have only words to play with," says Humbert, and only words can bridge the gulf suggested by Lolita's palm. Humbert has failed once—"She would mail her vulnerability in trite brashness and boredom, whereas I use[d] for my desperately detached comments an artificial tone of voice that set my own teeth on edge"—but it is a necessary act of love to try, and perhaps Nabokov succeeds with the reader where Humbert failed with Lolita.

Nabokov's account of the book's origin is fitting. "The first little throb of *Lolita,*" he writes,

> went through me late in 1939 or early in 1940, in Paris, at a time
> when I was laid up with a severe attack of intercostal neuralgia.
> As far as I can recall, the initial shiver of inspiration was some-
> how prompted by a newspaper story about an ape in the Jardin
> des Plantes who, after months of coaxing by a scientist, pro-
> duced the first drawing ever charcoaled by an animal: this sketch
> showed the bars of the poor creature's cage.

Humbert, the "aging ape" writing from prison, whose impossible love metaphorically connects him with that imprisoned animal, learns the language, in his fashion, and records his "imprisonment," and his book is the "picture" of the bars of the poor creature's cage. Yet from behind these bars, Humbert also exults. In *Gogol,* Nabokov notes how "one likes to recall that the difference between the comic side of things, and their cosmic side, depends upon one sibilant," a juxtaposition implicit in the early title, *Laughter in the Dark.* The title goes two ways: it records the laughter of the cosmic joker who has made a pawn of Albinus, blinding and tormenting him, but it also summarizes Nabokov's response to life, his course for survival. Towards the end of *Lolita,* the sick and despairing Humbert has finally tracked down Lolita, who is now the pregnant Mrs. Richard Schiller. He recalls how he rang the door bell, ready to kill Dick. The bell seems to vibrate through his whole exhausted system, but suddenly Humbert takes his automatic French response to the sound and playfully twists it into verbal nonsense: "*Personne. Je resonne. Repersonne.* From what depth this re-nonsense?" he wonders. It sounds from the depths of Vladimir Nabokov's profoundly humane comic vision; and the gusto of Humbert's narration, his punning language, his abundant delight in digressions, parodies, and games all attest to a comic vision that overrides the circumscribing sadness, absurdity, and terror of everyday life.

Lolita: The Quest for Ecstasy

Julia Bader

The form and movement of *Lolita* are shaped by a dual task: to record the emotional apotheosis of the narrator's passion for a nymphet, and to transform his story into a work of art which will immortalize that passion. Thus the question of the nature of artistic creation is posed directly by the witty pedant, obsessive pervert, and ecstatic lover whose personality and motivation constitute one of the implicit themes of his memoir. Humbert Humbert is constantly conscious of the difficulties of creating a vehicle adequate to his adored subject and to his purpose of explaining, justifying, and condemning his role in Lolita's life.

Although the novel is a memoir narrated in the first person, there are themes and revelations of which Humbert is not fully in control. The striking verisimilitude which Nabokov creates through the mask of Humbert is only one aspect of a shifting tale. Despite the sharpness of observation, the flawless ear for dialogue, the detailed evocation of everyday American scenes, Humbert attempts to manipulate his readers; and he is manipulated, in turn, without being aware of it. Critics have posed the question: "Is there a voice behind Humbert?" and have answered in the negative. But "point of view" need not be expressed through a separate voice; in Nabokov's case it is more a network of details behind and around Humbert which is not of his conscious making, and of which he may be unaware. After all, Aubrey McFate, the dramatization of destiny as decreed by the omniscient author, is not Humbert's agent; and Humbert himself, when Lolita reveals the name of her abductor, bows to a larger fictional necessity.

From *Crystal Land: Artifice in Nabokov's English Novels.* © 1972 by the Regents of the University of California. University of California Press, 1972.

In significant and easily recognizable ways *Lolita* is rooted in a realistic convention, a lifelike density which is one of its most pleasurable achievements. Humbert, too, has a certain consistency of tone and characterization: he does not fade into the papier-mâché backdrop, nor does he "peter out" to merge and disappear into his creator, as do most other Nabokovian main characters. The following remarks about the theme of art as suggested by and glimpsed through the narrative do not mean to deny the compelling presence of the realistic foreground, but point to an aspect of the novel wherein many of Humbert's aims and pronouncements converge with his desires.

As my analyses of *Sebastian Knight* and *Pale Fire* [elsewhere] have demonstrated, the theme of artistic creation runs through all of Nabokov's works, sometimes treated seriously, sometimes through parody. He enjoys combining the earnest declaration with its tongue-in-cheek counterpart; the true ecstasy with its mawkish replica. The intricate structure of *Lolita* comprises a number of themes and metaphors, all of which are fitted into the quasi-realistic American setting and yet extend the implications of Humbert's passion for nymphets into a treatment of the thrills of a butterfly hunt, the problems of a chess game, and assorted parodies of traditional and contemporary topics. Nevertheless, the theme of artistic creation deserves particular attention: an illuminating and pervasive motif throughout the book, it is reflected in the "moral apotheosis" of H. H., the role of Lolita, and the form of the entire novel. In view of a certain aspect of Nabokov's definition of fiction and art (as the realm where the norm is "ecstasy"), Humbert's obsession is best described as "artistic." The emotional intensity, coupled with the stylistic care which Humbert lavishes on his Lolita (and Nabokov on his *Lolita*), strives to attain a beauty and perfection which is closest to "aesthetic bliss."

In most of Nabokov's novels, the private vision of love creates a world of significance and value for the lover. The narrator of "Spring in Fialta," happily married, admits his "hopeless" love for another woman and thus understands "why a piece of tinfoil had sparkled so on the pavement, why the gleam of a glass had trembled on a tablecloth, why the sea was ashimmer: somehow, by imperceptible degrees, the white sky above Fialta had got saturated with sunshine, and now it was sun-pervaded throughout, and this brimming white radiance grew broader and broader." The illumination of the interior consciousness comes with the feeling for another being which results in a painful understanding of one's own isolation. The lover's passion is rarely reciprocated, nor is he allowed to rest in the joy of possessing his beloved.

Many of Nabokov's minor artists enact a search for the meaning of the relationship between fate and passion. The torment and elusiveness of this search is frequently represented through the symptoms of perversion and madness. But each artist-hero constructs private designs or quirky games which alleviate and approximate the anxieties and joys of his emotional life. Through his characters' absorption in a personal cult, Nabokov expresses the uniqueness of every personality.

Most of the time the hero is forced to rest in the torture of disunity, prey to the tricks of others as well as his own weaknesses. Yet there is a recurring element of beatitude in his torture. The Nabokovian lover relishes the twofold nature of reality, in which the vulgarly obvious and everyday object has a profundity and fineness available to him alone. His point of view is determined by the "reality" of his desire. Thus Lolita's conventionality throws Humbert's ideal view of her into sharper and more poignant relief, making his fantasy vision all the more precious by its precariousness. Lolita's shortcomings as a human being parallel the shortcomings of the literary form which depicts her. She has the same relation to the original Annabel of Humbert's youth as the finished novel has to its initial conception. Humbert describes his love for Annabel as a state where "the spiritual and the physical had been blended in us with a perfection that must remain incomprehensible to the matter-of-fact, crude, standard-brained youngsters of today." The fact that Lolita is presented largely as such a "youngster," and yet eclipses the sensitive sea-nymphet for Humbert, suggests that the imagination both relishes and transcends the physical world. The material for the imagination may lie in the physical world. But the product of the imagination is transformed into a passionately emotional object, which then lives independent of any conventional "reality." What H. H. overlooks until it is too late is the unique mystery in even such seemingly conventional characters as his nymphet.

In his *Nikolai Gogol,* Nabokov praises *The Government Inspector* (which he calls *The Government Specter*) for "blending in a special way different aspects of vulgarity so that the prodigious artistic merit of the final result is due (as with all masterpieces) not to what is said but to how it is said." Similarly, Nabokov finds that in *The Overcoat,* "the real plot . . . lies in the style, in the inner structure of this transcendental anecdote." So too in Nabokov's works, the narrator is often deliberately placed in conventional situations from a bildungsroman, a sentimental novel, or a mystery story. Instead of minimizing the traditional nature of such passages, Nabokov describes these scenes in exaggerated and self-conscious style.

Much of Humbert's imaginative creation is chronicled through such stylistic devices. His rival is repeatedly pictured as a "well-known" author, a purveyor of banalities and sham artistry: an exploiter of public shallowness, ignorance, and bad taste. The rival is sometimes the hero's clever, despised alter ego. He stages the conventional scenes in order to torment the hero, or to seduce the tantalizing, elusive woman who embodies both the emotional and artistic hopes of the protagonist. This theme is used also in Nabokov's early novel, *Laughter in the Dark*. The woman may be vulgar, mediocre, or shallow; but as Diana Butler notes in her persuasive essay on the butterfly theme in *Lolita:* "Nabokov tells us that the object of passion is unimportant, but that the nature of passion is constant."

At the same time, the self-mocking commentary of the narrators on their own passionate involvements, the self-conscious dissection by the author of his own work, and the shifting nature of the characters within each work suggest that there is no stable, empirical "reality" in which the object of passion and the lover can meet. Nabokov's way of constantly reworking and varying the theme of artistic creation reflects his belief that "verisimilitude" exists only in relation to imaginative landscapes, and that the final and unique "truth" about a novel lies in the artist's self-contained fictional construct. This attitude toward "reality" as something which is entirely controlled and fashioned by the author is an essential explanation of much of the mystification, maddening inconstancy, and continual character shifts which are so typical of Nabokov's novels. In answer to an interviewer's question about whether his characters ever "take hold" of him, Nabokov replied: "I have never experienced this. . . . I am the perfect dictator in that private world, insofar as I alone am responsible for its stability and truth."

The emphatically "private" nature of Nabokov's view of art and reality is paralleled in the novels by the jealously guarded unique obsession of many of the characters. The uniqueness of *Lolita,* of course, lies partly in its being a love story in which a vulgar, unromantic twelve-year-old is the object of passion, while her mother, full-blown and conventionally seductive, is viewed with distaste. While the theme of an affair between the lodger and the mother is an obvious cliché, the agonizing love for a slangy twelve-year-old is a delectable taboo. Throughout *Lolita* there is persistent identification between Humbert as lover and Humbert as artist, between the everyday, sentimental-novel existence of Lolita, and her mysterious Humbertian transformation: "Neither is she the fragile child of a feminine novel. What drives me insane is the twofold nature of this nymphet, . . . this mixture in my Lolita of tender dreamy childishness and a kind of eerie vulgarity, stemming from the snub-nosed cuteness of ads and magazine pictures . . . ; all this gets mixed up with the exquisite stainless tenderness seeping through the musk and the mud, through the dirt and the death, oh God, oh God! And what is most singular is that she, *this* Lolita, *my* Lolita, has individualized the writer's ancient lust, so that above and over everything there is—Lolita." Humbert later characterizes his writings as "nightmare curlicues . . . ; hideous hieroglyphics . . . of my fatal lust," and his first orgasm of vicarious pleasure is described as being "suspended on the brink of that voluptuous abyss (a nicety of physiological equipoise comparable to certain techniques in the arts)."

It is significant that Humbert can be near Lolita only by agreeing to a conventional marriage with the mother, just as earlier he married Valeria (whom he calls a "stock character") so as to overcome his abnormal yearning for nymphets. The disgust Humbert feels for these stylized, "normal big" women is the sexual counterpart of his scorn for banal sentiments and hackneyed use of language. His unquenchable desire for Lolita is identified with his search for a mode of expression which is mysterious, tender, alluring, at the same time that it is growing up into the conventional commonplace, for the use of pseudo-artists like Quilty. On one level, then, *Lolita* is a sustained attack on traditional literary banalities; interwoven with this parody of clichés, however, is the search for ecstasy which culminates in the achievement of sincerity and tenderness in human expression. Nabokov presents this search as inseparable from artistic sincerity and tenderness, and therefore his parody of genres is also a mocking exposition of shallow emotionality.

The foreword to *Lolita* is an obvious parody of the instructive appreciations that commonly preface works on controversial subjects. Thus "John Ray" gravely assures us that this is a "tragic tale tending unswervingly to nothing less than moral apotheosis." Much of the mock-preface is clearly ridiculous: not only the above invocation of "tragic" respectability, but also the condescending tolerance for Humbert Humbert, even though he is "abnormal" and "not a gentleman," and the insistence on the "general lesson" beneath the morbid details. Finally, "John Ray" patronizingly suggests that "this poignant personal study" should alert us to see beyond the twisted passion of Humbert Humbert to contemporary evils.

This foreword is an example of the versatility of Nabokov's humor. On the surface it is a parody of conventional prefaces, with their slick, serious, "openminded" evaluations. But Nabokov does not simply endorse the obverse of John Ray's opinions. The preface asserts the moralistic critical cliché that *Lolita* deals with the horrifying misery and consequences of perversion in order to affirm, obliquely, the value of morality, and to show the insidious threat to our ethical beliefs: "In this poignant personal study there lurks a general lesson; the wayward child, the egotistic mother, the panting maniac—these are not only vivid characters in a unique story: they warn us of dangerous trends; they point out potent evils." This is a parody of the insistence of critics that literature is not only a "story" but can be utilized as social commentary and moral guidebook. Yet Nabokov is implying not merely that this novel does nothing of the sort, but that, without knowing it, John Ray is telling the truth: that *Lolita* "warns us of dangerous trends," except that the warning is not moral or social, but rather aesthetic and literary. "The wayward child, the egotistic mother, the panting maniac" are, from an artistic point of view, not social evils, but evils of hackneyed characterization and theme in contemporary novels. Much of the irony of the preface lies in Ray's obtuseness in failing to recognize that the same "types" of characters are given the opposite roles from those which they play in conventional novels.

Nabokov's afterword to *Lolita*—which has a more subtle but nevertheless potent element of tongue-in-cheek discussion ("an impersonation of Vladimir Nabokov talking about his own book")—repudiates John Ray's declaration that the novel has a "moral" and asserts that the object of the work is to "afford" "aesthetic bliss." In comparing the modern pornographer with his eighteenth-century counterpart, Nabokov notes the "musts" of the twentieth-century work: "Action has to be limited to the copulation of clichés. Style, structure, imagery should never distract the reader from his tepid lust." If these rules are not adhered to, the modern pornographer runs the same risk as a detective story writer: that "the real murderer may turn out to be, to the fan's disgust, artistic originality." I contend that the "real perversion" in *Lolita* is artistic originality, and that when Nabokov complains of having had to abandon his "natural idiom," and being forced to do without "the baffling mirror, the black velvet backdrop, the implied associations and traditions—which the native illusionist, frac-tails flying, can magically use to transcend the heritage," he is incidentally giving us clues about his techniques of transcending the "heritage" of contemporary fiction.

The use of parody as literary criticism is interwoven with the other themes of *Lolita;* and it is possible, on one level, to regard the slangy, vulgar, irresistible nymphet as an embodiment of the possibilities inherent in the stock "wayward-child" character, or as an example of how "literary originality" can utilize a moral taboo for its subject. As I will try to show, moral taboo merges with literary taboo, and we get the supreme subject of literary originality posing as the main character of a novel about literary originality.

The parodic style is also an indirect mode of characterizing Humbert. Aside from the frequent statements on his madness or megalomania by Humbert himself, his seemingly rational descriptions of his reactions also indicate that he is perennially on the verge of insanity. His madness is sometimes the comic replica of a literary pose, as in the scene after he has received Charlotte's love letter:

> After a while I destroyed the letter and went to my room, and ruminated, and rumpled my hair, and modeled my purple robe, and moaned through clenched teeth and suddenly—Suddenly, gentlemen of the jury, I felt a Dostoevskian grin dawning (through the very grimace that twisted my lips) like a distant and terrible sun. I imagined (under conditions of new and perfect visibility) all the casual caresses her mother's husband would be able to lavish on his Lolita. . . . "To hold thee lightly on a gentle knee and print on thy soft cheek a parent's kiss. . . ." Well-read Humbert!

The techniques of love-making identified with literary techniques, Humbert's lust described as "the writer's ancient lust," the scenes of the novel referred to as a "dream," a "daymare," all point to a level of interpretation on which the action of the novel becomes metaphorical of the act of artistic creation. Indeed, it is possible to title this level of meaning, as Humbert suggests, "the portrait of the artist as a younger brute." Lolita herself exists on this plane as an ephemeral, ever-changing chief character in a projected work by an egomaniacal, alternately guilt-ridden and triumphant Humbert. Initially she is a potential fictional subject, existing in the unformed flux of the physical world, whose creation by Humbert simultaneously involves destruction. The twelve-year-old Dolores Haze lives in the everyday landscape of suburban America, mediocre and anonymous, until Humbert, with "a few madhouses behind him" and his nymphetic obsession before him, decides to invest her with a fictitious allure and build her into a work of art. The object of Humbert's search is avowedly illusory, and he knows that its glow will disappear by the time he has found and used her. He often compares his wooing of Lolita to a "game," or a "hunt," and the gradual numbness and unhappiness into which he transfixes Lolita also suggests the predicament of the artist, trying to capture his subject in the act of motion but succeeding only in divesting it of its vitality. Hence the persistent emphasis on Humbert's guilt, on the fading of Lolita's connection with everyday life, the growing bitterness and misery of their cohabitation.

Humbert experiences both pride and agony in seeing Lolita play tennis. She is used to playing childish games of volleyball against a neighboring wall, but Humbert has her take professional lessons in tennis; and watching her, he has "the teasing delicious feeling of teetering on the very brink of unearthly order and splendor." Humbert's obsession for her has forcefully molded the average Dolly into an "unearthly order" which shuts her off from the normal life of her contemporaries. Similarly, a cherished object of emotion may be abstracted and removed from its natural surroundings. Humbert's aesthetic obsession destroys the object of its attention; he watches the tennis game "with an almost painful convulsion of beauty assimilated." But Lolita has become the shell of her former self: she has a "form" which is "an absolutely perfect imitation of absolutely topnotch tennis," without any interest in the actual goal of the game. She has acquired the flattened, two-dimensional quality of an abused theme, and Humbert, in retrospect, sees that "had not something within her been broken by me—not that I realized it then!—she would have had on the top of her perfect form the will to win, and would have become a real girl champion." But Humbert has recreated Lolita in his own desire, and this new Lolita is sullenly but irrevocably dependent on him alone: "She had absolutely nowhere else to go."

Yet there remains a tantalizing part of Lolita which is resistant to the process of artistic abstraction, which constantly threatens to grow up and engulf the nymphet part. This stubborn streak is always contemplating escape, and responds shrilly to Humbert's love-making. And it is this streak which Humbert in the end comes to love. It is partly the streak of self-sustaining vitality in fictional characters which transcends and resists even their creator, the author himself.

The struggle between Humbert and Quilty is described as the "silent, soft, formless tussle on the part of the two literati," and the scene has a nightmarish unreality which reflects the state of mind of the dazed Humbert, who is blinded by his artificial world of hallucinatory images. As Lolita is trying to explain her aversion to him, Humbert silently supplies the words for her: "*He* broke my heart. *You* merely broke my life."

The novel abounds in references to literary form and devices, as if the ravages of Humbert's work were strewn all over the creative battlefield. Humbert has "used" the beautiful, trusting, American countryside, and in the process "defiled" it. Charlotte, the faithful "seal," has been eliminated, and Valeria and her husband were made to live as the degraded subjects of a scientific experiment. The bizarre, half-naked character who is found in Humbert and Rita's bedroom near the end of the book, claims that Humbert has "purloined" his identity, and he is renamed at the local asylum as "Humbertson." It is as if Humbert had toyed with the idea of developing him as a character, but had finally decided to leave him without identity. Several other characters are only half-developed: the neighbor in Ramsdale is simply called Miss Opposite, and an unnamed celebrity is referred to as Mr. Doublename (an early hint of Quilty). The main characters are suggestive of the creative process; their identities and defining qualities are constantly shifting. Quilty is amorphously present in Ramsdale, speaks in the dark of The Enchanted Hunters Inn, and slowly evolves from an amalgam of Uncle Gustave Trapp to a series of shadowy figures who trail Humbert in variously colored rented cars. Even these cars often acquire qualities suggestive of their driver—as at the Chestnut Crest garage, where "a red hood protruded in somewhat cod-piece fashion," a reference to Quilty's odious sexuality. Quilty's artificiality is further emphasized by his nickname, "Cue."

Humbert's theories of sex and of perception reveal a preoccupation with the intellectual uses of physical phenomena: "It is not the artistic aptitudes that are secondary sexual characters . . . ; it is the other way around: sex is but the ancilla of art." His vision is clouded by the urge to abstract the present and render it timeless: "You know—trying to see things as you will remember having seen them." Thus the flux of the moment is frozen into its interacting components, and becomes a disjointed tableau of details. He sees Charlotte's death in an "actual flash" of "sharp unity," but his analytical mind resolves it into a revelation of "the agent of fate," consisting of "intricacies of the pattern" which made up the physical event. Humbert's article on the mind proposes "a theory of perceptual time based on the circulation of the blood and conceptually depending . . . on the mind's being conscious not only of matter but also of its own self, thus creating a continuous spanning of two points (the storable future and the stored past)."

Humbert's mind gradually de-emphasizes "matter," and concentrates on a consciousness of its own self. Thus the two spanned points which operate between future and past are intertwined and frequently identified. For example, the shock of finding the tennis court empty suggests "Charlotte's face in death," and this past event is merged with two hypothetical present alternatives which appear as solid realities to Humbert: "I . . . noticed Lo in white shorts receding through the speckled shadow of a garden path in the company of a tall man who carried two tennis rackets. I sprang after them, but as I was crashing through the shrubbery, I saw, in an alternate vision, as if life's course constantly branched, Lo, in slacks, and her companion, in shorts." The alternate vision is not life's course, but rather the alternative suggested by the imagination, or by the process of artistic creation which deliberates between two possible representations of a particular scene. We are frequently given numerous possibilities or versions of a scene, just as we see shifting characteristics of Quilty, Humbert, and Lolita. The total impression is of a story which is in the act of being composed. Humbert himself is the most intricately developed character, and he is the mainspring of the action. If his vision is prismatic, so is the vision of the author who manipulates him. Thus we have the illusory representation of action as told by Humbert's journal, and the illusory existence of Humbert himself, as created by Nabokov.

The "intricate pattern" of conventional art is sometimes referred to as McFate, whom Humbert is constantly and unsuccessfully trying to outwit. "Precise fate" arranges Charlotte's death, which is actually a demand of the plot of the story, or a demand of the novel convention, to which the tortured Humbert surrenders his ideal passion. As Humbert comes to the end of his narrative, and looks back from the pregnant, ruined Dolly Schiller to the twelve-year-old misty Lolita, he realizes that the artistic process he glorified in the past, "what I used to pamper among the tangled vines of my hear, *mon grand péché radieux,* had dwindled to its essence: sterile and selfish vice." He had imposed his own obsession on the everyday physical world:

> Nothing could make my Lolita forget the foul lust I had inflicted upon her. Unless it can be proven to me . . . that in the infinite run it does not matter a jot that a North American girl-child named Dolores Haze had been deprived of her childhood by a maniac, unless this can be proven (and if it can, then life is a joke), I see nothing for the treatment of my misery but the melancholy and very local palliative of articulate art. To quote an old poet:

> > The moral sense in mortals is the duty
> > We have to pay on mortal sense of beauty.

A "mortal," constricted artistic awareness ("sense of beauty") produces a concern with morality. But the imagination which is not bounded by time or moral taboo has a "sense of beauty" which is independent of "reality" or morality. If the act of transforming and creating a nymphet from an ordinary child is retroactively seen by Humbert as a "sterile and selfish vice," it is the vice of the artist's sinister manipulation. Humbert's "sense of beauty" is heightened and purified after he has completed and "lost" his creation. The seventeen-year-old Lolita is no longer an object of obsessive lust ("all *that* I canceled and cursed"), no longer a resurrection of the ideal of the past (Annabel), but loved for herself, as she is in the present. "I insist the world know how much I loved my Lolita, *this* Lolita, pale and polluted, and big with another's child, but still grey-eyed, still sooty-lashed, still auburn and almond, still Carmencita, still mine."

Quilty (perhaps his name denotes the idea of his being a patchwork of a number of characters), as a rival, is a practitioner of thoroughly conventional art. He is a "public" author; he appears in cigarette ads and teenage magazines, and makes pornographic movies. He also "likes little girls," and the prison *Who's Who* informs Humbert that Quilty's "many plays for children are notable," such as *The Little Nymph* (in which Lolita plays the main character in the Ramsdale production). Quilty makes use of art in a cold, calculating way, he has no creative power (significantly, he confesses to Humbert that he did not enjoy Lolita because he is impotent); he uses Lolita for a brief scene and then discards her.

The amorphous figure of Quilty is a threat to the artistic integrity of Humbert's creation. As Humbert realizes that he is being pursued by Lolita's unknown seducer, he knows that the deadly struggle between his conception of art (as passion, lust, agonizing destruction of creator and object) and Quilty's dashing facility is being decided. The difference between the two men is a quality of seriousness and ecstasy, which Humbert sees dramatized in the chase on the highway "between our humble blue car and [his] imperious red shadow—as if there were some spell cast on that interspace, a zone of evil mirth and magic, a zone whose very precision and stability had a glass-like virtue that was almost artistic." Perhaps this is the zone which Humbert unsuccessfully tries to transcend in his attempt to save his ideal of Lolita from becoming crystallized in a standard artistic mode.

When Humbert hears Dolly Schiller identify Quilty as her abductor, he comments: "I, too, had known it, without knowing it, all along. . . . Quietly the fusion took place, and everything fell into order, into the pattern of branches that I have woven throughout this memoir with the express purpose of having the ripe fruit fall at the right moment; yes, with the express purpose of rendering . . . that golden and monstrous peace through the satisfaction of logical recognition, which my most inimical reader should experience now."

The "fusion" should be taking place in the reader's mind: the character of Quilty should merge into Humbert. Humbert supplies the clues for this fusion by emphasizing his own role as artist: "the pattern of branches that *I* have woven throughout this memoir" (italics added). The pattern has been anticipated and manipulated by Humbert, the "woven branches" are the action, dialogues, and characters of the novel. The stress on the deliberate artistic patterning ("with the express purpose of rendering") and the parody of conventional fictional expectations ("the satisfaction of logical recognition") serve to remind us in the midst of a "realistic" scene that Humbert is writing and arranging the story we are reading. The paradox of "I, too, had known it, without knowing it" might suggest that H. H., for novelistic purposes, had to *pretend* to his readers that he had not all along known about Quilty, or that H. H. here is hinting at his awareness of the omniscient author behind him, who has plotted the story from the start.

Humbert is master of the characters within the scope of his journal. He manipulates them according to his whim—except for the character of Lolita, who obsesses him. His vision reflects the manifold recesses of literary possibility. He ironically sees himself in the pose of the creative artist: "Humbert the Cubus schemed and dreamed—and the red sun of desire and decision (the two things that create a live world) rose higher and higher, while upon a succession of balconies a succession of libertines, sparkling glass in hand, toasted the bliss of past and future nights." His vision is directed at the image of illusion within illusion, as his constant references to mirrors and lakes suggest. His fantasy spans the past and the future. The potentiality of perfection lures him on in his painful affair with Lolita—but her essence, which is rooted in the present, eludes him.

We cannot ascertain whether Quilty is actually following their car, or whether the "clues" of the hotel registers were really diabolically planted by Quilty. What is important is that Humbert is driven to the edge of madness by the effort to preserve Lolita in his own image, and the guilt and shame of his irreparable tampering with her magic serve to point to his inability to attain the perfect literary "equipoise" between her movement in everyday life and her immobile existence in the realm of art. Humbert is perennially toying with shifting scenes and dialogues: the enactment of the final murder scene with Quilty is the amalgam of numerous versions of murders culled from Humbert's dreams and hallucinations. This may account for the nightmarish, unreal quality of the final scene, as if Humbert had not quite decided how the scene should take place, and is experimenting with a dummy Quilty to determine the best posture and the most suitable number of bullets.

Humbert constantly hears unsaid echoes of conversations, and this gives the impression that the unused lines which he has decided to eliminate from the final version are still lingering behind the irrevocably "used" ones. At The Enchanted Hunters Inn, Humbert has a conversation with a still uncreated Quilty, to whom he has decided to give a voice, but not a name or a face. Even the act of "creating" Quilty's voice is dramatized: "The rasp of a screwing off, then a discreet gurgle, then the final note of a placid screwing on. . . . His voice addressed me: 'Where the devil did you get her?' 'I beg your pardon?' 'I said: the weather is getting better.' " Humbert mentally adds "stillborn babies" to a motel's otherwise innocuous list of things not to be flushed in the toilet; his description of himself fluctuates between Humbert the Wounded Spider and Humbug the Giant Killer.

He is gradually enveloped by the consequences of his desecration, at first only as a vague hint, later as a perpetual shadow. Still at the beginning of their romance, he retroactively sees himself and Lolita in a symbolic relationship: "She was sprawling and sobbing, and pinching my caressing hand, and I was laughing happily, and the atrocious, unbelievable, unbearable, and, I suspect eternal horror that I know now, was still but a dot of blackness in the blue sky of my bliss."

Perhaps Quilty serves partly to dramatize Humbert's ritualistic killing of pseudo-art, which has defiled his own passionately loved art object. It is not until Humbert decides to kill Quilty that the playwright actually begins to "exist." Humbert the artist sees that the plot necessitates Quilty's appearance, and "in the methodical manner on which I have always prided myself, I had been keeping Clare Quilty's face masked in my dark dungeon, where he was waiting for me. . . . I have no time right now to discuss the mnemonics of physiognomization." Apparently Humbert does not leave himself enough time to do a thorough characterization, because he describes the about-to-be-eliminated Quilty as "this semi-animated, subhuman trickster."

In sharp contrast to the half-emerging characters around her, Lolita is described in minute detail: her smell, her mannerisms, her thigh and arm measurements are given with meticulous precision. But only too late does Humbert realize that he has given her no soul, that in spite of his painstaking artistry he has failed to appreciate her wonder and mystery, and it shocks him to the border of unconsciousness to think that "I simply did not know a thing about my darling's mind, and that quite possibly, behind the awful juvenile clichés, there was in her a garden and a twilight, and a palace gate."

Humbert's awareness of the peril of his artistic attempt makes him a jealous guardian of Lolita, both to protect himself and to keep her from being soiled by the "dirty children who were her contemporaries." After she has left him, Humbert finds that she has broken something in him: "One essential vision in me had withered: never did I dwell now on possibilities of bliss with a little maiden, specific or synthetic . . . ; never did my fancy sink its fangs into Lolita's sisters, far, far away, in the coves of evoked islands." He is still dominated by the compulsion to track down Lolita and Quilty, but he knows that he can derive no happiness from indulging in his monomania. He has given up the dream of actualizing the phantoms of the imagination, phantoms which were initially "perfect, just because the vision was out of reach, with no possibility of attainment to spoil it by the awareness of an appended taboo; indeed it may well be that the very attraction immaturity has for me lies . . . in the security of a situation where infinite perfections fill the gap between the little given and the great promised—the great rosegray never-to-be-had." This description corresponds to Humbert's "pre-dolorian past," when the promise of attaining the ideal was made by Annabel. "Since I sometimes won the race between my fancy and nature's reality, the deception was bearable. Unbearable pain began when chance entered the fray and deprived me of the smile meant for me. . . . The radiant foreglimpse, the promise of reality, a promise not only to be simulated seductively but also to be nobly held—all this, chance denied me—chance and a change to smaller characters." The terminology of drama and print ("smaller characters"), along with a hint of the omniscient author's control ("chance"), is used to express Humbert's sense of the circumscribed nature of his world and of his imaginative range.

If Humbert sees a "succession of balconies with a succession of libertines" (the libertines being the multiple reflections of his lustful self, refracted in the process of re-creation), so Nabokov sees a succession of Humberts on shifting fictional levels. Gaston, the lovable, harmless pervert, and Quilty, the witty, vulgar, commercial nympholept, dramatize extremes of Humbert's varied personality. The novel builds up and undermines its "realistic" illusion, presenting a succession of characters on a succession of mimetic levels. While Humbert frequently appears to be the sole creator of his narrative, various details, acts of McFate, flutterby inserts, and the shadow extending from the foreword point to the author who created Humbert. Within the narrative sequence of the theme of creation, Humbert, the passionate but minor author, loses control of his main character and becomes a slave to her in the act of abusing her; his lust gives way to tenderness when he realizes that affection is the mainspring of creation. (This realization, which takes place during Humbert's visit to Dolly Schiller, is foreshadowed by the school play in which Lolita acts, though the play is a parodic distortion of the "outer" novel's action.) Whether or not we are to "believe" Humbert's final conversion and declaration of love does not seem to me to be an issue in the novel. The element of surprise, of the contradiction and inconsistency joyfully embraced and passionately asserted, becomes metaphoric of the artist's relationship to his material. Humbert's unconventional obsession is a necessary aspect of imaginative transformation, and his acceptance of his love for the grown-up Lolita provides for his moral apotheosis into the realm of art.

Humbert to the end remains partly destructive and ludicrous (Nabokov's moral condemnation always hovers around Humbert's rhetoric), but he is allowed the saving recognition that feeling is primary and that grace springs from love lavished on illusory or alien objects. On the level of the art theme, *Lolita* deals with the complexities of a fictional world, with certain artistic problems in the portrayal of imaginative reality, a consideration which is already at least once removed from the philosophical problem of perceiving reality. The questions tackled by *Lolita* are artistic, or aesthetic, and the "moral" dilemma is treated in aesthetic terms. Humbert's "vice" is the inexpert artist's brutal treatment of a tantalizingly undeveloped subject, whose fragile soul Humbert has violated. The grossest violation is Quilty's, the commercial artist's, and his crime is so monstrous that it merits the greatest punishment in a novel about artistic creation: he is left deliberately half-created.

What Nabokov, living in his workshop "among discarded limbs and unfinished torsos," attempts to achieve is an artistic triumph related to the basic problem of fiction. Humbert observes that "we are inclined to endow our friends with the stability of type that literary characters acquire in the reader's mind. . . . Never will Emma rally, revived by the sympathetic salts in Flaubert's father's timely tear. Whatever evolution this or that popular character has gone through between book covers, his fate is fixed in our minds. . . . Any deviation in the fates we have ordained would strike us as not only anomalous but unethical." But Humbert, weaving in and out of madness, treating Lolita with alternate cruelty and ecstasy, has no "stability of type." He has been deliberately created to embody the metaphoric perversion and contradictions inherent in the desire to possess and to create. The journal he writes reflects this instability, and we will never know how much of his life was coincidence, how much of it chance, how much of it the cruel machinations of a rival. Whether he is mad or not, whether he imagined the entire story of his affair with Lolita, is not answered by the book. His complexities are the embodiments of artistic problems and of the creative process. His fantasy-life is indistinguishable from his "real" life. The characters he encounters, the conversations he records, cannot be checked against a yardstick of "what really happened." Nabokov, in creating Humbert, has attempted to write a book in which the characters are infinitely fluid, and the action takes place on a "succession" of fictional planes, so that the characters cannot be finally "stilled" or "fixed" as being particular "types," whose fate is sealed forever within the confines of the covers of the book.

Nabokov lightly foregoes the obligation to give us all the necessary information about the characters or the nature of the action. He has "transcended the heritage" of the author's responsibility for providing final answers, or defining the limits of his work. Humbert's obsession is the pursuit of ecstasy through artistic creation. This quest for a pattern within his obsession is conveyed by various metaphors for the act of writing. These metaphors often assume a "realistic" aura, at least momentarily, but eventually they fuse into the creating mind of Humbert. The despair, shame, agony, and tenderness with which Humbert fashions the figure of Lolita is the subliminal journey in the novel. It is a journey through the mind of a mad yet lucid memoirist whose tale reveals artistic as well as emotional agony. In the act of tracing this perverted quest for ecstasy, the omniscient author creates an allusive web beyond his hero's awareness. Artistry and perversion thus enact a quasi-realistic drama of verbal gaiety and emotional intensity. This heightened drama illuminates the undercurrents, both playful and agonizing, of the literary process.

L*olita* and Pure Art

Michael Bell

One of the dangers of trying to read literature seriously, and one that is increased in the ambience of academic professionalism, is that the reader's inevitable and proper desire to "ériger en lois ses impressions personelles" is so easily and fatally reversible. The result is that literature itself is subtly deprived of its particular weight and meaningfulness by the discussion of more general issues into which it gets absorbed. The reader's response begins to derive from his commitment to a general theoretical position rather than the other way round. Critical discussion of Nabokov, to the extent that it takes place at all, is especially prone to this. The *TLS* review of Alfred J. Appel's *The Annotated Lolita,* indicates that, for all the academic ink expended on Nabokov's novels, reasoned judgements about specific literary quality are rare. Where the heat built up by the exegetical industry of the Nabokovian meets the cooler scepticism of the non-Nabokovian there may be a rumbling of thunder but little clearing of the air. The argument quickly becomes an appeal to general principle rather than to the work itself. The following passage from the review exemplifies this, I think, fairly enough:

> But this edition is not going to convert those critics who find in
> Nabokov's self-conscious funning merely poverty and nasty tri-
> fling; it is not the moralist or the addict of novelistic realism who
> needs to be persuaded. The central doubt about Nabokov, and
> even more about Nabokov criticism, is that the value of self-
> consciousness seems to be taken for granted and the tone and

From *Essays in Criticism* 24, no. 2 (April 1974). © 1974 by Stephen Wall.

texture of people, events and cultures become matters of more
or less distant allusion. This is not a moralist's objection, as
Professor Appel seems to think: indeed his "proof" that *Lolita* is
not pornographic might be taken to sever its last links with any
kind of vitality. In erecting Nabokov's technique into the *content*
of the book, what his editor has here produced is the kind of arid
paradox that repels so many readers:

> "The word involution may trouble some readers, but one has
> only to extend the dictionary definition. An involuted work
> turns in upon itself, is self-referential, conscious of its status as a
> fiction, and *allégorique de lui-même*—allegorical of itself, to use
> Mallarmé's description of one of his own poems. An ideally
> involuted sentence would simply read, 'I am a sentence.'"

The critical deadlock illustrated here is not, of course, entirely the fault of
the commentators: the problem is precipitated by Nabokov himself, both in
his novels and in the principles of taste expressed in his own *obiter dicta* on
literature generally. Indeed, I think it is part of a larger problem in assessing
the literature of the last couple of decades that works of fiction frequently
and legitimately raise theoretical, not to say philosophical, issues that are
more interesting than the works themselves. One might extend the argument about Nabokov to embrace a whole body of contemporary writing
predicated, like his, on the absolute value of fiction. However, in the so-
phistical atmosphere of academic letters the reader needs to appeal from
criticism to experience, and to consider the book itself apart from, or even
in opposition to, the more general and ready-made significances and pro-
fundities which he may be cajoled into bringing to it. In the specific case of
Lolita it seems to me that in its overall structure the novel itself attempts to
resolve the deadlock exemplified by Appel and his reviewer.

The novel does this by modifying the basic terms of the argument.
While *Lolita* indeed "allégorique de lui-même," and hence comparable to a
Mallarmé poem, it is indicative that the example appealed to should be a
poem rather than another work of fiction. The traditional bias and strength
of the novel form has been its minute and extensive depiction of common
experience. I think a traditional experiential freight of this kind in *Lolita* sets
up a resistance to the novel's overt aesthetic isolationism. In doing so it does
not undermine or impede, or even just provide a platform for, this aesthetic
dimension but instead crucially modifies its meaning. The distinction we
commonly draw between art and life refers mainly to two distinct kinds of

objects, those we encounter within imaginatively created frames and those we do not, but (as everyone recognises) the human observer of a work of art actually belongs simultaneously to both worlds in a state of mind so essentially mysterious that it has eluded abstract definition from Plato to the present. I think Nabokov's *Lolita* does something different from, and more important than, what either Appel's or his reviewer's accounts seem to assume. It does not simply isolate itself in a world of aesthetic "game"; it rather uses that game as the context in which to embody dramatically, and in doing so to justify humanly, precisely that elusive state of emotion and insight in which the apparently polar elements of the special aesthetic perception and common experience are inextricably and mysteriously merged. The book itself works to supplant the absolutist terminology in which it is often discussed.

I do not claim to know to what extent this view of *Lolita* may correspond to any intention Nabokov actually had in writing it; his own recorded comments are concerned to make a very different emphasis, and Appel is no doubt true to the spirit of his author. I am concerned rather to suggest what the book yields when viewed from a different standpoint. However carefully it may be contained in a spirit of parody or play, the book engages our interest in the game itself by exciting a sense of the human values it is playing with. What I value in the novel is something that possibly Nabokov himself would not, but which I see as part of the overall logic of the book's conception and in fact enriching, rather than denying, its Nabokovian spirit. The intentional nettle must however be grasped since it is precisely the programmatic self-consciousness of the novel, its overt commitment to a view of art, that occasions the dispute. Nabokov's own statement, in the remarks appended as an afterword to later editions of *Lolita,* that he seeks only "aesthetic bliss" in a novel, coupled with the many allusions to Flaubert in *Lolita* itself, suggests the larger background of the dispute: it is a variation of the continuing modern argument about the meaning of the "Flaubertian" aesthetic. It may be useful, therefore, to reconsider briefly Flaubert's own aspirations and practice insofar as these throw a comparative light on Nabokov and other contemporary "fabulators." It is also more fruitful, if we wish to compare Nabokov with another writer fascinated by the notion of "pure" art, to pursue the comparison with a novelist rather than a poet.

Flaubert is like "God in creation" not only in the sense of his own definition (later endorsed by Joyce's Stephen Dedalus) that as artist he is "everywhere felt, but nowhere seen," but also in the Voltairean sense that if Flaubert had not existed, modern criticism would have had to invent him.

In fact the term "Flaubertian" as commonly used is to some extent an invention of criticism, since it refers to an attitude simpler than that actually espoused by Flaubert. It is most readily associated with such well-known statements on the autonomy of the art-object as:

> What I should like to write, is a book about nothing, a book dependent on nothing external, which would be held together by the strength of its style, just as the earth, suspended in the void, depends on nothing external for its support.

Yet for all this preoccupation with formal perfection, Flaubert's letters also make frequent and sympathetic reference to artistic values directly opposed to those for which he is now proverbial. He admires the apparently free-flowing, "artless" energy of the great artists of the past:

> Still, one thing is depressing, and that is to see how easily the great men achieve their effects by means extraneous to Art. What is more badly put together than much of Rabelais, Cervantes, Molière, and Hugo? But such quick punches! Such power in single word! We have to pile up a lot of little pebbles to build our pyramids; theirs, a hundred times greater, are made with a single block. But to seek to imitate the method of those geniuses would be fatal. They are great for the very reason that they have no method.

Even if we approach Flaubert's private statements (such as his avowed humility here) with something of the circumspection we would doubtless bring to Nabokov's public ones, there remains a tangible and important difference between Flaubert's assertion of the principle of artistic autonomy and that of many of his modern successors. The new region of Art had not yet been settled or charted and his declarations of intent function more like compass bearings than territorial enclosures. The modifying element in his aesthetic aspiration is exemplified in the sudden change of direction at the end of another famous passage:

> I remember how my heart throbbed, and what violent pleasure I experienced, when I looked at one of the walls of the Acropolis, a wall that is completely bare (the one to the left as you climb the Propylaea). Well, I wonder whether a book, quite apart from what it says, cannot produce the same effect. In a work whose parts fit precisely, which is composed of rare elements, whose surface is polished, and which is a harmonious whole, is there

not an intrinsic virtue, a kind of divine force, something as eternal as a principle?

But then, a few lines later:

> If I were to keep going very long on this track I should find myself in a hopeless predicament, for Art must also come from the heart. Or rather, Art has only those qualities that we can give it; and we are not free. Each of us follows his path, independent of his own will.

The final reservation indicates that although the ideal already expressed is seen to be strictly unattainable, it is nevertheless meaningful in that the very pursuit of it gives a different spirit to the whole. And the passage makes clear that Flaubert's admiration for those "unartistic" geniuses, such as Cervantes, is not a parenthetical respect for something with no direct application to his own Art. *Madame Bovary* is enough to demonstrate that the artist's own, largely involuntary, humanity or "heart" is the ultimate basis for great art. The force of Flaubert, both in his major novel and in his aesthetic perceptions, lies largely in his straddling a divide between an older moralistic tradition and his own ideal of "pure" art. He comprehends each with a deeper appreciation, rather than one at the expense of the other. Hence, when mid-twentieth-century writers express apparently comparable aesthetic aspirations we may question whether they have this broader human fullness in which Flaubert's Art is rooted; particularly since after Joyce and Flaubert himself one might expect such aestheticist principles to require less insistent affirmation. In a general way, it seems to me that the sense of tragic paradox that informs Flaubert's attitude to Art has been diluted in the contemporary fabulator to a bland assurance. I think, however, that Nabokov, at least in *Lolita,* does evince this further dimension but in a manner different from Flaubert, and in some ways more subtle, precisely because the Joycean/Flaubertian strain is so thoroughly assimilated into twentieth-century literary sensibility. *Lolita,* close in theme to the vulgar and unhappy loves of Emma Bovary, is almost a stock-taking for what has happened to this strain of sensibility between our time and Flaubert's.

This shift in the nature of aestheticist aspirations between Flaubert's time and Nabokov's is paralleled in their fiction. For Flaubert this absolute commitment to Art was still an awesome matter, not to be invoked casually or in any but the most serious jest. And the sense that his aesthetic perspective was unique infuses the work itself; in *Madame Bovary* the stylistic fastidiousness through which the characters are viewed implies a highly exclusive mode of sensibility. As with Joyce later, all the energies of the work, comic, satiric and tragic, are generated by the polarity between the quality of the material and the quality of the observation—a polarity very different from the moral superiority of, say, George Eliot to her characters. Joyce and Flaubert set them against, not the warm sympathy of an author, but the glittering impersonality of the artefact. But what appears in Flaubert, and already less so in Joyce perhaps, as an exclusive or aristocratic authorial perspective has, by the mid-twentieth century, become sufficiently demo-cratised to be the likely possession of any educated man; Flaubert himself is now part of the general cultural heritage. And so Nabokov's Humbert as a mid-century, educated *homme sensuel* is a character embodying at once the emotional vulgarity and folly of Emma Bovary *and* the Olympian fastidi-ousness of her creator.

In the light of this historical perspective we might, then, summarise the dispute about *Lolita* in the following manner. Does Nabokov's combining in one character the polar elements that constitute the Flaubertian or Joycean mode, have the effect of merely creating a short circuit as the critical view referred to by the reviewer in effect suggests; or does it, as Appel might argue, create within the closed circuit a beautiful display against the back-drop of cosmic darkness; or is there the further possibility that power is there and is being used for more than its own self-delight, however philo-sophically resonant we may see that as being? I think the last suggestion is the truer one but it should be admitted that the first is to some extent justified, or at least that this is the danger the book inevitably courts. In Flaubert's rendering of Emma Bovary's limited and sentimental world there is a substantial human freight, a poignancy, that Nabokov's account of Humbert and Lolita does much to emulate. But as we move away from these central characters to figures like Quilty the solipsistic trickiness of the book begins to take its toll. The thinness here, by more traditional novelis-tic standards, is not attributable simply to the execution, nor to my drawing an unfair comparison with a greater writer such as Flaubert; it is implicit in the work's conception. The pyrotechnics of the novel at such points are certainly dazzling but they form a display in which the eye must be willing-ly induced to accept the emptiness behind the show. In other words, it is where the book is most squarely based on Appel's kind of aesthetic principle that it is most vulnerable to the reviewer's reservations.

But the gradual emergence of a body of character and action that resists the psychologically "realistic" apprehension initially invited by Lolita and Humbert plays a role in the novel different from what one might expect if it were described in isolation. It does not have the effect found in Flann

O'Brien's *At Swim-Two-Birds* in which the author's exuberant inter-involvement of different levels of narrative "reality" undermines the "realistic" potential of the characters for the sake of a formal game that, entertaining as it initially is, seems to have less and less idea what to do with itself. In *Lolita* the firm control of the game within the mind of Humbert himself at the time of writing, and the peculiar interrelations of the Humbert/Lolita/Quilty triangle, mean that the elements of formal game and "realistic content" are not only able, as in *Tristram Shandy,* to coexist but to do so in a mutually illuminating light. Humbert's dual role as character and author, and his simultaneous relations with the psychologically realistic character of Lolita on the one hand and with the overtly contrived character of Quilty on the other, superimpose the worlds of fiction and life to embody and define an emotional state, and moral viewpoint, that cannot exist without some elements of both worlds. This makes possible a definition of "art" emotion in the living context that we recognise as part of the larger meaning of art. Or we may look at this proposition from the other side, for in *Lolita,* as in the classic bildungsroman, the hero's emotional and moral growth is inseparable from his growth in the understanding of aesthetic principles. The reason Humbert's story has not the immediate appearance of a bildungsroman is that, apart from flashbacks to his adolescent relationship with Annabel, he is a mature and sophisticated man from the beginning of the story, with considerable literary and artistic experience. Yet this familiarity with literature and art is precisely the way in which the essential point is made that he does not possess this experience in the true spirit. He has knowledge and apparent sophistication but lacks true understanding until the very end of his relationship with Lolita.

Although in this sense *Lolita* is the story of Humbert's aesthetic education, the manner in which he matures differs from the usual patterns of the bildungsroman and indeed from the more customary modes of fiction generally. Whereas the novel, and especially the bildungsroman, characteristically shows a growth in understanding through assimilating a body of experience, in Humbert's case the emphasis falls on the attainment of a spiritual standpoint which up till then neither formal education and culture nor common experience has apparently been able to teach him; once acquired, it transforms his personality. This spiritual change is more analogous to a religious revelation than to the slower processes of education; it seems to come finally in a sudden realisation and from outside his normal view of experience, even though it works in large measure through the everyday world and can eventually transform it. The departure from a purely "realistic" narrative frame in *Lolita* signals a transforming psychological dimension, just as similar tricks in Muriel Spark's *Memento Mori* more obviously suggest a supernatural spiritual dimension. In both cases there is a perspective introduced that is not readily derivable from more "normal," earthbound views of life. The peculiar relation between the "realistic" narrative and the authorial "games" in *Lolita,* then, expresses the relation between these two dimensions of experience: they remain distinct yet inter-involved. The passage from one to the other seems to need a difficult spiritual leap and yet, once the leap has been made, there seems to be no point at which they can be picked apart. The second is a transforming, not a simple supplanting, of the first.

The difference that comes over Humbert in the course of the novel, his spiritual leap, may conveniently be defined (in the terms of Joyce's Stephen Dedalus) as a move from a kinetic to an aesthetic attitude in his feeling for Lolita. In Stephen's case much of his priggishness comes from his too early and generalised espousal of the aesthetic attitude; he gives insufficient thought to whether or not one's fellow beings are the proper recipients of one's aesthetic emotions. Humbert's problem is the reverse, since his emotions for certain young girls are almost totally kinetic; what he needs is the capacity for a more impersonal relation to his own feelings and their human objects. The crucial point is that neither the kinetic nor the aesthetic can usefully be regarded as being in some general way preferable to the other. The more comprehensive desideratum is rather to have the saving capacity for impersonal contemplation, where appropriate, of even those emotions by which we act on our fellow beings.

Of course, the change in Humbert's feelings for Lolita from seeing her lubriciously as a sexual object to seeing her eventually as a person, has a grounding in psychological realism, particularly in the final episode of his meeting with her as wife and expectant mother. But his way of assimilating the emotional crisis this occasions is by drawing on the emotional standpoint of the latent artist in himself. This shows itself in two principal ways: firstly, in his consciously facing and killing Quilty whom, as the parodic tone of the whole episode indicates, he now sees as his artificially or fictionally contrived double rather than simply as his literal rival; secondly, of course, in the subsequent writing of the story that is to become *Lolita.* In short, he meets the emotional crisis within the story by placing himself half outside the narrative frame—the writing of the story placing him within a frame and the treatment of Quilty helping to move him out of it. Humbert's ability at this point to be both within and outside the frame rises naturally from the mode of narration employed throughout which, by its tonal liberties and games, always superimposes the Humbert of the writing on the earlier Humbert of the events. This overall strategy is capable of significant use only because the Humbert of the story has the latent but convincing ability to be the creator of the fiction—an ability that provides the continuing thread of his emotional and aesthetic education.

This thread, though initially thin, is tenacious. The early part of Humbert's narrative is based not simply on his memory but also on the diary he kept while at the Haze house, so that we have not just an earlier and later Humbert, but an earlier and later writer. We might describe this diary as not merely kinetic, but (to continue with Stephen's terms) as actually pornographic. Like a scribbling on a jakes wall, it expresses the unrealisable or public unadmissible desire at a fairly simple and crude symbolic remove from actual fulfilment. And yet, as connoisseurs of such graffiti will testify, even that unpromising context can provide scope for a play of wit and a grosser kind of artistry. Humbert, at this stage, seems to have a comparable ambivalence. He is able to stand sufficiently outside his own feelings to pursue their object with caution and to have a sense of the ironies of his position, but he cannot, or does not wish to, escape or even consider the implications of his compulsions. In short, he can be wittily cynical where necessary, but not impersonal about himself in the sense of giving equal imaginative sympathy to another.

This ambivalence of the early Humbert as one in some degree capable of self-detachment but using this ability in a totally kinetic spirit is neatly and ironically caught in his relations with Charlotte Haze; she in effect provides him, in his capacity as creator of fictions, with his first public. When he is first settling into married life with her she obliges him to exchange stories with her of their former "love-lives," his being fictitious and hers genuine. Humbert goes on to observe that her accounts

> were, ethically, in striking contrast with my glib compositions, but technically the two sets were congeneric since both were affected by the same stuff (soap operas, psychoanalysis, and cheap novelettes) upon which I drew for my characters and she for her mode of expression.

He is sufficiently aware of the different status of life itself and its fictional models to be able to manipulate the fiction to deceive Charlotte and further his own ends. By the same token, the deception is only possible because of Charlotte's habitual and total naivety in viewing fiction so kinetically and realistically that she cannot distinguish it from actuality even in her own immediate experience. Poor Charlotte, the absolute dupe of the fictional manipulation of imagination and desire, hence provides a double comment on Humbert: he is indeed technically more sophisticated than she, but uses that capacity in a way that, just like her naivety, distorts its spirit. It is an appropriate irony, then, that when Charlotte finally discovers his diary she should be perfectly right in not believing his explanation that it was the working draft of a novel merely making use of the names and situation of the Haze household.

Humbert's education in the symbolic handling of emotion, by which he progresses from pornographic cynicism to genuine impersonality, is conducted largely by the two characters who are to him respectively human individual, and fellow—or rival—artist: Lolita and Quilty. Lolita, partly under the direction of Quilty, lays the more subtle and less overt ground-work for Humbert's aesthetic education. She relates to him in a dual way that expresses the central dilemma of the book: she is both an object and a person to him. But the formal strategy of the book derives from this duality a more complex and less sentimental conclusion than any such straightfor-ward moral proposition as that we should strive to treat our fellow beings as persons rather than as objects. Lolita is an object to Humbert for most of the novel in the sense that it is essentially a reworking of the Pygmalion story; Humbert is from the beginning quite explicit about the unreality of the Lolita he is creating as the object of his desire. As the ironically exotic nickname itself implies, she is being quite distinct from the actual Dolores Haze who is the necessary condition of her existence. The name, "Haze," along with all the other metaphors of delusive vision, suggests the con-sciously nurtured illusion by which she is created. As Humbert puts it bluntly enough in an early episode: "Lolita had been safely solipsised." From here on, as with Shaw's use of the Pygmalion story, the artificial woman created for purely personal reasons by her male creator asserts an increasing independence until the project simply disappears into the person. At the same time, however, there is a countermovement: Lolita escapes the domination of Humbert by herself deliberately becoming an artist of sorts. It is not simply the warm humanity of the person, then, that subverts his inhuman view of her. On the contrary, as he has made an object of her in enslaving her, she now escapes him by voluntarily creating that object for him. Having learned through Quilty something of the art of acting, she carries this over completely into her life with Humbert. Incidentally, she herself thereby learns what her unfortunate mother never knew: the dif-ference between an actual and a romanticised or fictitious self. And her subsequent marriage, though undeniably bleak, has nonetheless a strength and realism to it that can be largely attributed to this rather brutal emotional education. Even though she does not tell Dick Schiller the complete truth about herself, this reserve itself expresses a realistic integrity in her relation with him and constitutes a beneficient contrast to Humbert's deceptive manipulation of her mother. More important for present purposes, though, is her effect on Humbert. His discovery that she has been deceiving him from within the very terms of his own solipsistic view of her is not only an emotional shock to him as a lover; it also forces him to arming it from within. . . . She asserts her otherness not, as we might have expected, by battering at his solipsism from the outside, as it were, but by penetrating and completely disarming it from within. Only when the imaginatively created object thus evaporates can he finally see the person. Since he has so well prepared for the recaltricance or indifference of the outside world to the satisfaction of his desires by making over everything into his own terms, this double attack, by which she smuggles her reality into his private world, seems the necessary way to face him with a tangle of emotions that refuse to be so compartmentalised.

The fact that the main characters are all artists of sorts gives meaning to the overall structure of the novel. While Humbert is being brought to recognise the humanity of Lolita, so the whole perspective through which she is being seen—that is, the novel itself—is being consciously reified into an aesthetic object. The realisation of her humanity hence occurs within the context of a more radically impersonal contemplation of her, himself and the whole relationship than he has ever been capable of before. The emergence of a fictional frame within the novel but around the Lolita story means that the mixed emotions and attitudes that constitute Humbert's initial response to Lolita can now be clearly delineated as belonging on one side or other of the frame. Hence he is finally able to respond to her as a person with a genuine, unself-regarding tenderness within the frame, only when the potentially dehumanising view of her as an object has found its proper context too: namely in the standpoint of the artist. It is not, then, that the awareness of others as "objects" is in itself wrong, but that it has to find its proper place in our general sense of them. From being initially projected by him as a quality of Lolita herself, it gradually moves outside the fictional frame altogether to become what it should be: a partial and necessary function of Humbert's mind.

This seems the most useful application of Nabokov's later resistance to moralistic readings of the novel. It does not seem to me to be true of *Lolita* to suggest, as Appel's remarks appear to, that it is totally isolated in a self-regarding, "aesthetic" void; the kind of moral significance it has is rather bound up with the value of the human capacity for disinterested and aesthetic contemplation of the emotional life and its human objects. Actually,

Nabokov's own gloss on his phrase "aesthetic bliss" seems to come pretty close to this " . . . a sense of being somehow, somewhere, connected with other states of being where art (curiosity, tenderness, kindness, ecstasy) is the norm." Art here is not seen in opposition to "tenderness" and "kindness" but is a special way of conceiving them. The novel itself seems to me to demonstrate in practice what this special way can mean. Humbert communicates this as much in the manner as the "content" of his account. In attaining an overtly "aesthetic" viewpoint, of which the spirit of game is an extreme expression, he justifies the art of Nabokov himself.

The interplay of psychologically realistic narrative and formal pyrotechnics in the book undermines conventionally moralistic assumptions of the narrower kind, and suggests that the instinct for art and game is as primary and salutary in the whole moral economy as feeling and impulse. Humbert's Nabokovian mischievousness is content to make local witty reversals of conventional wisdom as in his remark; "It is not the artistic aptitudes that are the secondary sexual characters as some shams and shamans have said; it is the other way round: sex is but the ancilla of art." But the overall structure of the book establishes a mutual interdependence of personal feeling and aesthetic impersonality more delicate than any simple reversal indictates. The simplistic extremes are all ultimately eschewed. If the "heart" alone is an uncertain guide to happiness, the spirit of heartless detachment, even for an "artist," is an equal if not greater human limitation. The emotionally naive Charlotte is matched at the other extreme by the heartless, manipulative "artistry" of Quilty. Only in Humbert's final state of mind, before his own much abused heart gives way, do we see the proper balance, the poignantly poised emotional fullness, to which the novel's overall structure gives elaborate adumbration. Where Flaubert admitted that Art must grow out of "heart" as well as the exigencies of "pure" form, his sombre view of life found mainly a polar relation between them. Nabokov's more positive or absolute view of the significance of artistic form has, at the risk of being merely charming in its dependence on formal funning, reworked the Flaubertian pattern so as to give the author's perspective to the character.

If it is agreed that this novel does formally bear such a reading, the critical question that remains is to what extent a work so conceived can actually survive its own trickiness. At a general level one can say that there are works, such as Joyce's *Ulysses* or Mann's *Doktor Faustus,* that earn the right to be read in their own way. The test can only be the practical one of whether the work makes this adjustment worthwhile, whether it enriches or impoverishes the book's life. To my mind the interest of *Lolita* is not simply the Nabokovian game, but the interaction of this game with the "human" material on which it is predicated. It is perhaps significant that, like those other great games with the world of fiction *Don Quixote* and *Tristram Shandy,* this novel is named after the character rather than simply the formal idea. Pure game is probably as difficult to achieve as pure art, and it is correspondingly difficult to determine with works that professedly seek such purity what exactly one is responding to when one responds sympathetically. Flaubert seems to have had a nose for the artistic fact where it diverged from, or was larger than, the artist's principle. *Lolita* creates a final state of mind that resists either a purely "aesthetic" formulation or moralistic reduction; in this respect it may be compared to the apparent banality of Quilty's dramatic offering on the same theme. The work is therefore something more than a "mere" game, and the readers who have a principled and exclusive commitment to either an "aesthetic" or a "moral" rationale for the novel are likely to miss what is most valuable in it.

Parody and Authenticity in *Lolita*

Thomas R. Frosch

It has been said that *Lolita* is simultaneously "a love story and a parody of love stories" and that its parody and its pathos are "always congruent." In this article I wish to explore what such a condition—that of being both parodic and authentic at the same time—may mean.

First, however, I suggest that we best describe *Lolita* generically not as a love story or a novel of pathos but as a romance. The plot itself is composed of a series of typical romance structures, each one a version of the quest or hunt and each one an embodiment of a specific type of suspense or anxiety. We begin with the pursuit of Lolita, and the anxiety of overcoming sexual obstacles. Next, once Humbert and Lolita are lovers, we have a story of jealousy and possessiveness, as Humbert is beset by fears of rivals and by Lolita's own resistance. Finally, in Humbert's dealings with Quilty, we have a third and fourth type, each with its attendant style and anxiety: the double story and the revenge story. Furthermore, these plot structures are infused with the daimonic (that is, a quality of uncanny power possessed originally by beings, whether good or evil, midway between gods and people), which is a primary characteristic of romance as a literary mode. Lolita is an inherently unpossessable object; her appeal consists partly in her transiency—she will only be a nymphet for a brief time—and partly in her status as a daimonic visitor to the common world. The quest is thus an impossible one from the outset; it is variously presented as a quest for Arcadia, for the past, for the unattainable itself; it is nympholepsy. Even in the rare moments when Humbert is free from his typical anxieties, he is not

From *Nabokov's Fifth Arc,* edited by J. E. Rivers and Charles Nicol. © 1982 by the University of Texas Press.

totally satisfied; he wants to "turn my Lolita inside out and apply voracious lips to her young matrix, her unknown heart, her nacreous liver, the sea-grapes of her lungs, her comely twin kidneys." Humbert is a believer in the enchanted and the marvelous. Like Spenser's Red Cross Knight, he rides forth on his quest adorned by the image of his guiding principle, in his case a blue cornflower on the back of his pajamas—the blue cornflower being Novalis's symbol of infinite desire. *Lolita* contains numerous parodic allusions to other literary works, especially to Mérimée's *Carmen* and Poe's "Annabel Lee," but the real anti-text implied by the allusions and parodies together is the romantic sensibility in general from Rousseau to Proust.

But exactly how seriously are we meant to take Humbert and his quest? The book's complexity of tone and the question of Humbert's reliability as a narrator are the first issues in an investigation of the relationship between the parodic and the authentic.

Nabokov takes great delight in rapid and unpredictable changes in tone; we are never permitted to rest for long in the pathetic, the farcical, the rapturous, or the mocking. One of the clearest examples of tonal complexity is the novel's "primal scene," the seaside love scene with Annabel Leigh. After a buildup of high erotic suspense during which the two children are repeatedly frustrated in their sexual attempts, the famous episode concludes as follows: "I was on my knees, and on the point of possessing my darling, when two bearded bathers, the old man of the sea and his brother, came out of the sea with exclamations of ribald encouragement, and four months later she died of typhus in Corfu." We misread this little rollercoaster ride from the impassioned to the hilarious to the poignant if we take any one of its tonalities as definitive. Certainly this is not simply a satire of the romantic; its effect comes rather from the coexistence of its three tonalities in a single moment. In such a passage, we might expect the romantic to go under, partly because of its inherent vulnerability and partly because, as the dominant tone of the long buildup, it is apparently punctured by the intrusion of the burlesque. Yet the paragraphs that follow return to a tone of erotic rapture in a scene that is chronologically earlier than the seaside scene. The second scene, describing another frustrated tryst, concludes as follows: "That mimosa grove—the haze of stars, the tingle, the flame, the honeydew, and the ache remained with me, and that little girl with her seaside limbs and ardent tongue haunted me ever since—until at last, twenty-four years later, I broke her spell by incarnating her in another." If Nabokov had intended to puncture Humbert's rhapsody, it would have been more appropriate for him to arrange the two scenes chronologically so that the ribald bathers would appear at the end of the entire sequence, instead of in the middle. As it is, nothing is punctured; if anything, the romantic has found a new energy after the interruption. It is as if, in the following paragraphs, the romantic has been given the bolstering it needs to be able to hold its own with the jocular.

The novel's narrative point of view is as elusive as its tone. Clearly, when Humbert tells us, as he does repeatedly, that he has an essentially gentle nature and that "poets never kill," he is belied by the destruction he wreaks on Charlotte, Quilty, and Lolita. And when Humbert accuses Lolita of "a childish lack of sympathy for other people's whims," because she complains about being forced to caress him while he is spying on schoolchildren, Nabokov is being sarcastic. Humbert also fails to see things that the reader can pick up; for example, he misses the name Quilty (*"Qu'il t'y"*) concealed in a friend's letter to Lolita. Just as clearly, though, Humbert is sometimes Nabokov's champion, as for example in Humbert's satirical comments about psychoanalysis and progressive education. At other points, Nabokov's attitude toward his persona is quite intricate: Humbert says of his relationship with Annabel that "the spiritual and the physical had been blended in us with a perfection that must remain incomprehensible to the matter-of-fact, crude, standard-brained youngsters of today"; and Humbert does serve as a serious critic of modern love from the standpoint of a romantic exuberance of feeling, even if his criticism is undercut by his own divided love, in which what he calls his "tenderness" is always being sabotaged by what he calls his "lust."

But if we compare Humbert to another demented storyteller in Nabokov, Hermann in *Despair,* we see how Nabokov operates when he really wants to make a dupe out of his narrator. *Despair* is a takeoff on the doppelgänger theme, in which the hero, Hermann, takes out an insurance policy on himself and then murders his double in order to collect; it doesn't work, however, because he's the only one who sees the resemblance. Hermann is among other things a Marxist, a sure sign that Nabokov is using him ironically, and Nabokov puts into his mouth frequent and obvious reminders of his unreliability. "I do not trust anything or anyone," he tells us. His wife's hero worship of him is one of his constant themes, and yet his self-satisfaction and blindness are such that he can find her undressed in the apartment of a man who is her constant companion and not experience a moment's doubt of her fidelity. Nabokov himself, calling both Humbert and Hermann "neurotic scoundrels," does make an important distinction between them, when he writes that "there is a green lane in Paradise where Humbert is permitted to wander at dusk once a year; but Hell shall never parole Hermann."

Even Hermann, however, at times seems a stand-in for Nabokov, as, for instance, whenever he speaks of outwitting or playing games with the reader. Much has been written of Nabokov's own fondness for game playing, such as the use of the *Carmen* parallel in *Lolita* to tease the reader into believing that Humbert will kill his nymphet. In fact, it's difficult to find a Nabokov hero or narrator, however antipathetic, who doesn't at times sound like the author in his nonfiction. Even John Ray, the fool who introduces *Lolita,* asserts a prime Nabokov theme when he says that every great work of art is original and "should come as a more or less shocking surprise." And many readers have noticed the relationship between the desperate nostalgia of Humbert or that of the crazed Kinbote in *Pale Fire* and Nabokov's own commitment to the theme of remembrance. Conversely, Van Veen in *Ada*—who is the Liberated Byronic Hero, among other things, as Humbert is the Enchanted Quester and Hermann the Metaphysical Criminal—although he has been taken as almost a mouthpiece for Nabokov himself, has been condemned by his creator as a horrible creature. The fact seems to be that Nabokov in his fictional and nonfictional utterances has created a composite literary persona, just as Norman Mailer has. His heroes, like Mailer's D. J. and Rojack, tend to be more or less perverse or absurd inflections of his own voice. In two of his own favorite works, *Don Juan* and *Eugene Onegin,* we have narrators who keep intruding on their heroes to deliver speeches and who also are at pains to differentiate themselves from those heroes. Nabokov behaves similarly, except that he does so within the range of the single voice. As in the case of tone, we discover an interplay of engagement and detachment, an interplay that is most active and subtle in the most memorable of the characters, like Humbert and Kinbote.

With this general sense of the status of tone and narrator in *Lolita,* we can turn now to consider what Humbert actually says. Humbert subtitles his story a confession. More accurately, it is a defense. Portraying himself as a man on trial, Humbert repeatedly refers to his readers as his jury. "Oh, winged gentlemen of the jury!" he cries, or, "Frigid gentlewomen of the jury!" But he also frequently addresses us directly as readers; in the middle of a torrid sequence he speculates that the eyebrows of his "learned reader . . . have by now traveled all the way to the back of his bald head." And late in the book, in a parody of Baudelaire's "Au lecteur," he addresses the reader as his double: "Reader! *Bruder!*" The reader is sitting in judgment on Humbert; the purpose of his story is to defend what he calls his "inner essential innocence"; and the rhetoric of the book as a whole, its strategy of defense, is proleptic, an answering of objections in advance. Humbert's self-mockery, for example, has to be understood as a proleptic device, and, indeed, to follow the style of *Lolita* is to track the adventures of a voice as it attempts to clear itself of certain potential charges. As we will see, in many ways the defense is Nabokov's, even more than Humbert's.

At the end of the novel, Humbert sums up his defense by passing judgment on himself; he would give himself "at least thirty-five years for rape" and dismiss the other charges, meaning chiefly the murder of Quilty. But there are further accusations that the novel strives to evade. As a whole, the book defends itself against a utilitarian concept of art. This charge is rather easily evaded by the use of John Ray, who introduces the novel as an object lesson in the necessity of moral watchfulness on the part of "parents, social workers, educators." Nabokov's obvious satire here is intended to remove the allegation of his having a conventional moral purpose. Other accusations are handled within the text itself. In addition to conventional moralists, Nabokov detests psychiatrists and literary critics, and it is against these types of readers—or these metaphors for the reader—that Humbert wages constant war. Anti-Freudianism is one of Nabokov's pet themes, and Humbert is a man who, in his periodic vacations in insane asylums, loves nothing more than to take on a psychiatrist in a battle of wits. His chief defense against a psychoanalytic interpretation of *Lolita* is to admit it readily and dismiss it as trite and unhelpful. When he describes his gun, he says, "We must remember that a pistol is the Freudian symbol of the Ur-father's central forelimb;" Humbert beats the analysts to the draw and says, in effect, "So what?" At another point, he anticipates a Freudian prediction that he will try to complete his fantasy by having intercourse with Lolita on a beach. Of course he tried, Humbert says; in fact, he went out of his way to look for a suitable beach, not in the grip of unconscious forces but in "rational pursuit of a purely theoretical thrill"; and when he found his beach, it was so damp, stony, and uncomfortable that "for the first time in my life I had as little desire for her as for a manatee."

Ultimately, we have to understand Nabokov's anti-Freudianism in the context of a hatred for allegory and symbolism in general. In *Ada,* Van Veen says of two objects that both "are real, they are not interchangeable, not tokens of something else." Nabokov is against interpretation; an image has no depth, nothing beneath or behind or beyond; it is itself. Discussing Hieronymus Bosch, Van tells us, "I mean I don't give a hoot for the esoteric meaning, for the myth behind the moth, for the masterpiece-baiter who makes Bosch express some bosh of his time, I'm allergic to allegory and am quite sure he was just enjoying himself by crossbreeding casual fancies just for the fun of the contour and color." Another of Nabokov's heroes, Cincinnatus in *Invitation to a Beheading,* is a man whose mortal crime is to be opaque, or inexplicable, while everyone else is transparent. To be inexplicable is to be unrelatable to anything else; Humbert refers to the "standardized symbols" of psychoanalysis, and Hermann, a bad literary critic, points out a resemblance that nobody else can see. Nabokov's hero-villains are often allegorists, like Humbert, who imposes his fantasy of Annabel Leigh on Lolita and turns her into a symbol of his monomania.

Allegory, as Angus Fletcher has shown, is daimonic and compulsive; it is a spell, enchanted discourse. Nabokov, on the contrary, tries to create structures that defy interpretation and transcend the reader's allegorism, Freudian or otherwise; like Mallarmé, he dreams of a literature that will be allegorical only of itself. Thus, Humbert evades our attempts to explain him according to prior codes or assumptions. First of all, he insists that women find his "gloomy good looks" irresistible; therefore, we can't pigeon-hole him as someone forced into perversion by his inability to attract adult women. Then, too, Lolita is not "the fragile child of a feminine novel" but a child vamp who, furthermore, is not a virgin and who, even further, Humbert claims, actually seduces him—a claim that is at least arguable. And finally, when we are forced to compare Humbert to Quilty, a sick, decadent, and cynical man, a man who is immune to enchantment, it becomes impossible simply to categorize Humbert as a pervert like all others. In all these ways, Humbert is not only made to look better than he otherwise would; he is also made difficult to explain and classify, and his uniqueness is a crucial theme of his defense. In *Ada,* Van Veen acclaims the "individual vagaries" without which "no art and no genius would exist." In *Despair,* Hermann the Marxist longs for the "ideal sameness" of a classless society, where one person is replaceable by another while his rival, the artist Ardalion, believes that "every face is unique." In fact, even Hermann admits that his double resembles him only in sleep or death; vitality is individuation. It is a favorite theme of Nabokov. We are told in *Pnin* that schools of art do not count and that "Genius is non-conformity." The author himself always hates being compared to other writers: Spiritual affinities have no place in my concept of literary criticism," he has said. In light of this, it is worth noting that the alienation and linguistic eccentricity of a character like Pnin are, in addition to being poignant and comical, the valuable signs of his singularity. Whatever else they are, heroes like Pnin, Humbert, and Kinbote are recognizable; they are rare birds. Humbert tells us that he is even singular physiologically in that he has the faculty of shedding tears during orgasm.

Humbert's chief line of defense is that he is no "brutal scoundrel" but a poet. Nympholepsy is aesthetic as well as sexual; the nymphet in the child is perceived by the mind. Humbert does not wish merely to tell us about sex, which anyone can do; he wants "to fix once for all the perilous magic of nymphets"; he wants to fix the borderline between "the beastly and beautiful" in nymphet love. He calls himself "an artist and a madman, a creature of infinite melancholy"; he is an explorer of that special romantic domain of sensation, the feeling of being in paradise and hell simultaneously; and he is a sentimentalist who revokes the anti-romantic bias of modernism in a sentimental parody of Eliot's *Ash-Wednesday*. The problem is that in portraying himself as a romantic dreamer and enchanted poet, rather than as a brutal scoundrel, he leaves himself open to another charge: literary banality. He recognizes his position as a spokesman for values that no one takes seriously anymore and says that his judges will regard his lyrical outbursts and rhapsodic interpretations as "mummery," so much hot air to glorify his perversion. His nymphet, on the other hand, is at best bored by his mummery, and the two often operate as a vaudeville team, in which he is the alazon and she the eiron:

> "Some day, Lo, you will understand many emotions and situations, such as for example the harmony, the beauty of spiritual relationship."
> "Bah!" said the cynical nymphet.

Humbert fears Lolita's "accusation of mawkishness," and his madcap and mocking humor defends him against any such accusation by the reader. So too does the presence of Charlotte, a trite sentimentalist whose mode of expression he mocks and against which his own appears unimpeachable. Yet he says, "Oh let me be mawkish for the nonce. I am so tired of being cynical."

If the book's central rhetorical figure is prolepsis, its central structural figure is displacement or incongruity. Often cultural or geographical, incongruity appears in such local details as Charlotte's calling her patio a "piazza" and speaking French with an American accent; but more generally it appears in Humbert's old-world, European manner—aristocratic, starchy, and genteel—set in a brassy America of motels and movie magazines, and in his formal, elegant style of speaking posed against Lolita's slang. But Humbert is not only out of place; he is also out of time, since he is still pursuing the ghost of that long-lost summer with Annabel Leigh. The incongruity is also erotic, in the sexual pairing of a child and an adult and, in the application of romantic rhetoric to child molesting, it appears as a problematic relation between word and thing. The geographical, linguistic, and temporal aspects of Humbert's dislocation are often related to Nabokov's own exile; but I wish to emphasize here another primal displacement, Humbert's status as a nineteenth-century hero out of his age. In this literary dislocation, a romantic style is placed in a setting in which it must appear alien and incongruous. Humbert's problem is to defend his romanticism in a de-idealizing, debunking, demythologizing time.

In *Eugene Onegin* Tatiana wonders if Onegin is a mere copy of a Byronic hero:

> who's he then? Can it be—an imitation,
> an insignificant phantasm, or else
> a Muscovite in Harold's mantle,
> a glossary of other people's megrims,
> a complete lexicon of words in vogue? . . .
> Might he not be, in fact, a parody?

Humbert, in his displaced and belated romanticism, must prove that he is not an imitation. Nabokov's use throughout his work of various doubles, mirrors, anti-worlds, and reflections has been much documented and explored. His heroes are typically set in a matrix of doubleness: the condemned man Cincinnatus in *Invitation to a Beheading,* for example, is doubled both by his secret inner self—his freedom or his imagination—and by his executioner. Among its many functions, the double serves as a second-order reality, or parody. The double Quilty parodies Humbert who parodies Edgar Allan Poe. Humbert is referred to many times as an ape, and an ape is not only a beast but an imitator. Nabokov has written that the inspiration of *Lolita* was a story of an ape who, when taught to draw, produced a picture of the bars of his cage. So Humbert, the ape, the parody, gives us a picture of his emotional and moral imprisonment and enchantment. To be free is to be original, not to be a parody.

"I am writing under observation," says the jailed Humbert. Once upon a time, observers walked out of the sea to destroy the best moment of his life; before their arrival, he and Annabel had "somebody's lost pair of sunglasses for only witness." Fear of discovery is Humbert's constant anxiety; he feels that he lives in a "lighted house of glass." The observer, the jury, the brother in the mirror represent the reader and also the self-consciousness of the writer. Robert Alter has pointed out in his excellent study *Partial Magic* that an entire tradition of the "self-conscious novel," stemming from *Don Quixote,* employs a "proliferation of doubles" and mirror images to present a fiction's awareness of itself as fiction and to speculate on the relation between fiction and reality. *Lolita* certainly participates in this tradition, but the sense of time expressed by its displacements and its literary allusions suggests that we understand its self-consciousness as specifically historical, as in the theories of Walter Jackson Bate and Harold Bloom. Humbert's jury is the literary past, which sits in judgment over his story. Humbert is both a mad criminal and a gentleman with an "inherent sense of the *comme il faut*"; self-consciousness figures here as the gentleman in the artist, his taste or critical faculty, his estimation of what he can get away with without being condemned as an imitator, a sentimentalist, or an absurdly displaced romantic.

What is on trial, then, is Humbert's uniqueness and originality, his success in an imaginative enterprise. To what judgment of him does the book force us? Quilty is the embodiment of his limitations and his final failure. He first appears to Humbert in the hotel where the affair is consummated; thus as soon as the affair begins in actuality, Humbert splits in two; and later, practicing to kill Quilty, he uses his own sweater for target practice. Described as the American Maeterlinck, Quilty is a *fin-de-siècle* decadent and thus the final, weak form of Humbert's romanticism; his plays reduce the themes of the novel to the sentimental and the banal: the message of one of them is that "mirage and reality merge in love." Quilty, who is worshipped by Lolita and who couldn't care less about her, incarnates the ironies of Humbert's quest: to possess is to be possessed; to hunt is to be hunted. In addition, to be a parody, as Humbert is of a romantic Quester, is to be defeated by doubleness: Quilty is an ape who calls Humbert an ape.

In relation to Lolita, Humbert accepts complete guilt. The end of the book is filled with outbursts against himself for depriving her of her childhood. A poet and a lover of beauty, he finishes as a destroyer of beauty. At one point, learning how to shoot, Humbert admires the marksmanship of John Farlow, who hits a hummingbird, although "not much of it could be retrieved for proof—only a little iridescent fluff"; the incident aptly characterizes Humbert's actual relationship to his own ideal. At the end, he recognizes that "even the most miserable of family lives was better than the parody of incest, which, in the long run, was the best I could offer the waif." All he can achieve is parody. When he calls himself a poet, the point is not that he's shamming but that he fails. Authenticity eludes him, and he loses out to history. What he accomplishes is solipsism, a destructive caricature of uniqueness and originality, and he succeeds in creating only a renewed sense of loss wherever he turns: of his first voyage across America with Lolita, he says: "We had been everywhere. We had really seen nothing. And I catch myself thinking today that our long journey had only defiled with a sinuous trail of slime the lovely, trustful, dreamy, enormous country."

Humbert is finally apprehended driving down the wrong side of the road "that queer mirror side." This is his last dislocation and is symbolic of all of them. We can now address one further form of displacement in Humbert's quest, the displacement of the imagination into reality. The mirror side of the road is fantasy, and Humbert has crossed over. Lolita was a mental image, which Humbert translated into actuality and in so doing destroyed her life and his; but his guilt is to know that she has a reality apart from his fantasy. The narrator of Nabokov's story " 'That in Aleppo Once. . . ,' " measuring himself against Pushkin, describes himself as indulging in "that kind of retrospective romanticism which finds pleasure in imitating the destiny of a unique genius . . . even if one cannot imitate his verse." So Humbert is proud to inform us that Dante and Poe loved little girls. Hermann, in *Despair,* treats the artist and the criminal as parallels in that both strive to create masterpieces of deception that will outwit observers and pursuers; it is Hermann's failure not only to be found out but to be told that his crime, an insurance caper, was hopelessly hackneyed. Kinbote too confuses imagination and reality in *Pale Fire,* for he thinks he has written a critique and a factual autobiography, whereas he has really produced a poem of his own. Crime and mythomania are parodies of art; Humbert parodies the novelist who attempts to displace the imagination into actuality, and this would seem to be the judgment of him handed down by the novel itself. Note, however, that this is the way romantic heroes—for example, Raskolnikov, Frankenstein, Ahab—typically fail. Perhaps it is Humbert's deeper failure to think, not that he could succeed, but that he could achieve the same kind of high romantic failure as those heroes of a lost age.

In any case, at the end, Humbert—who was a failed artist early in his career, who tried to translate art into life and again failed, and who then turned a third time to art, now as a refuge, a sad compensation, and a "very local palliative"—sees art as a way to "the only immortality" he and Lolita may share. Having in effect destroyed her, he now wants to make her "live in the minds of later generations." A new idea of art does begin for him in his own imaginative failures. Then, too, he now claims to love Lolita just as she is, no longer a nymphet and now possessing an identity, dim and gray as it may be, that is separate from his private mythology. Thus, unlike Hermann, who will never be paroled from Hell, Humbert is finally able to see beyond the prison of his solipsism.

At this point I wish to turn from Humbert's engagement with the parodic and the romantic to Nabokov's, and I will begin with several points about parody in general. Parody is representation of representation, a confrontation with a prior text or type of text. The mood of the confrontation varies with the instance. We can have parody for its own sake; for example, in *TLS* (January 21, 1977), Gawain Ewart translated an obscene limerick into two prose passages, one in the style of the *OED*, the second in the style of Dr. Johnson's dictionary. Then we can have parody for the purpose of critique—satirical parody, such as J. K. Stephen's famous takeoff on Wordsworth and his "two voices": "one is of the deep . . . And one is of an old half-witted sheep." *Lolita* includes examples of both types: for instance, the roster of Lolita's class with its delightful names (Stella Fantazia, Vivian McCrystal, Oleg Sherva, Edgar Talbot, Edwin Talbot . . .) and the Beardsley headmistress's spiel about her progressive school ("We stress the four D's: Dramatics, Dance, Debating and Dating"). But as a whole the novel participates in a third type, parody that seeks its own originality, what Robert Alter would call metaparody: parody that moves through and beyond parody.

When Alter calls parody "the literary mode that fuses creation with critique," he is saying something that is strictly true only of satirical parody. What is common to all three types is that they fuse creation with differentiation. Parodists use a voice different from their own in such a way as to call attention to themselves. Parody is at once an impersonation and an affirmation of identity, both an identification with and a detachment from the other. This sense of displaced recognition, this incongruous simultaneity of closeness and distance, is a primary source of the delight and humor of parody, although it should be noted that parody is not inevitably comic, as in the case of John Fowles's *The French Lieutenant's Woman,* for example. Some parody, such as Stephen's, emphasizes the distance, but we also need to remember John Ashbery's idea of parody to "revitalize some way of expression that might have fallen into disrepute." It may be true that some aggression is inherent in all parody, no matter how loving, but it is an aggression that is more primal than intellectual critique: it is the kind of aggression that says, "This is me. This is mine."

Page Stegner has said that Nabokov uses parody to get rid of the stock and conventional, and Alfred Appel, Jr., that he uses parody and self-parody to exorcise the trite and "to re-investigate the fundamental problems of his art." I think it is finally more accurate to say that he uses parody to evade the accusation of triteness and to elude the literary past in the hope of achieving singularity. Nabokov's parodism is an attempt to control literary relations, a way of telling his jury that he already knows how his book is related to prior work. More than that, it is a way of taking possession of the literary past, of internalizing it. Nabokov has repeatedly noted and critics—most vividly, George Steiner—have often stressed the idea that he writes in a borrowed language. But in his difficult condition of personal and linguistic exile, Nabokov also points to another, more general kind of displacement. Irving Massey has suggested that many works of literature deal with the problem that "*parole* is never ours," that we all speak a borrowed idiom in expressing ourselves in the public medium of language. It is also relevant that a writer inevitably speaks in the borrowed language of literary convention. Like so many other writers of the nineteenth and twentieth centuries, Nabokov dreams of detaching his representation from the history of representations, of creating a *parole* that transcends *language*.

In relation to romance, parody acts in *Lolita* in a defensive and proleptic way. It doesn't criticize the romance mode, although it criticizes Humbert; it renders romance acceptable by anticipating our mockery and beating us to the draw. It is what Empson calls "pseudoparody to disarm criticism." I am suggesting, then, that *Lolita* can only be a love story through being a parody of love stories. The most valuable insight about *Lolita* that I know is John Hollander's idea of the book as a "record of Mr. Nabokov's love affair with the romantic novel, a today-unattainable literary object as short-lived of beauty as it is long of memory." I would add that parody is Nabokov's way of getting as close to the romantic novel as possible and, more, that he actually does succeed in re-creating it in a new form, one that is contemporary and original, not anachronistic and imitative. Further, it is the book's triumph that it avoids simply re-creating the romantic novel in its old form; for Nabokov to do so would be to lose his own personal, twentieth-century identity.

Nabokov has tried to refine Hollander's "elegant formula" by applying it to his love affair with the English language. His displacement of the formula from the literary to the linguistic is instructive. Indeed, both in theory and practice, he is always moving the linguistic, the stylistic, and the artificial to center stage. "Originality of literary style . . . constitutes the only real honesty of a writer," says Van Veen, who characterizes his own literary activities as "buoyant and bellicose exercises in literary style."

Language that calls attention to itself relates to romance in one of two ways. Either it becomes—as in Spenser or Keats—a magical way of intensifying the romance atmosphere, or—as in Byron with his comical rhymes and his farcical self-consciousness—it demystifies that atmosphere. As in *Don Juan,* language in *Lolita* is used to empty out myth and romance. The novel opens with Humbert trilling Lolita's name for a paragraph in a parody of incantatory or enchanted romance language and proceeds through a dazzling panorama of wordplay, usually more Byronic than Joycean: zeugmas, like "burning with desire and dyspepsia"; puns, such as "We'll grill the soda jerk"; alliterations, such as "a pinkish cozy, coyly covering the toilet lid";

unexpected and inappropriate condensations, such as the parenthetical comment "(picnic, lightning)" following Humbert's first mention of his mother's death; instances of language breaking loose and running on mechanically by itself, as in "drumlins, and gremlins, and kremlins"; monomaniacal distortions of diction: "adults one dollar, pubescents sixty cents."

Certainly, verbal playfulness for its own sake is an important feature of Nabokov's art; certainly, too, we ought not underestimate the way in which Nabokov's linguistic exile has contributed to his sense of language as an objective presence, not merely a vehicle. It may also be that wordplay is used to overcome language: in *Despair,* Hermann says that he likes "to make words look self-conscious and foolish, to bind them by the mock marriage of a pun, to turn them inside out, to come upon them unawares." But I would suggest that language is finally a false clue in Nabokov's work unless we see that his centering of language and style chiefly has the value of a poetic myth. A literature of pure language and convention is a dream, congruent with the dream of a literature beyond interpretation; it is a dream of literature as a word game with no depth, a manipulation of conventions, a kind of super-Scrabble. The function of this poetic myth, or "bellicose exercise," is here proleptic; it detaches the writer from the romantic so that he may then gain for the romantic an ultimate acceptability.

This is also true of the idea of games in Nabokov and of all the devices of self-consciousness that Alfred Appel, Jr., has valuably described, such as the kind of coincidental patterning that runs the number 342 into the novel in different contexts to emphasize the artificiality of the fiction. Humbert and Quilty share with their creator a love for the magic of games, as do so many other of Nabokov's characters; and sometimes that magic can assume diabolical form, as it does in the case of Axel, a forger of paintings and checks in *Laughter in the Dark.* The vicious Axel completely identifies creativity with game playing; for him, "everything that had ever been created in the domain of art, science or sentiment, was only a more or less clever trick." Parody, Nabokov has said, is a game, while satire is a lesson. A game is a matter of manipulating conventions; it is also a matter of play, a little Arcadia; and it is also a matter of competition. We can look at the idea of the game as a trope, a clinamen in Harold Bloom's sense, by which Nabokov swerves from the dead-seriousness of typical romance. But I see it ultimately, like parody and the centering of style, as an enabling poetic myth, the I-was-only-joking that permits us to get away with shocking utterances, like romantic rhapsodies in the mouth of an urbane, sophisticated, literate person like Humbert. It is the fiction that permits fiction to occur.

We might say that Nabokov must kill off a bad romantic and a bad artist in Humbert in order for his own brand of enchantment to exist. Nabokov's recurrent fascinations are romantic ones; he writes about passion, Arcadia, memory, individualism, the ephemeral, the enchanted, imagination, and the power of art. Indeed, his problem in *Lolita* is essentially the same as Humbert's: first, to be a romantic and still be original, and, second, to get away with being a romantic. *Lolita* has been taken as a critique of romanticism, and I am not arguing that it should be read as a romantic work. Rather, in its final form it is a work of complex relationship to romanticism, a dialectic of identification and differentiation. Like Byron in *Dón Juan,* Nabokov in *Lolita* is divided against himself, although in a different way: Byron is a poet struggling against his own romantic temperament, while in Nabokov we see a romantic temperament trying to achieve a perilous balance in an unfriendly setting. But the results do illuminate each other: in *Don Juan* a romantic lyricism and melancholy are achieved through mocking parody and farce; in somewhat similar fashion, Nabokov uses the energies of his style—its parody, its centering of language, its flamboyant self-consciousness—first against the spirit of romance and then in behalf of it. This, then, is the status of style in *Lolita,* and this is why style is elevated to such prominence; perhaps this is even why it must be a comic style: it functions as a defensive strategy both against the romanticism of the material and against the anti-romanticism of the "jury."

Indeed, the tradition of romance continues most interestingly and convincingly today in writers, such as Thomas Pynchon and John Fowles, who are ambivalent about it and often present it negatively. In such teasing and parodic works as *V.* and *The Magus* we see an attempt to gain the literary power of romance without falling under its spell. These are romances for a demythologizing age. The phenomenon of the romantic anti-romance is hardly new; *Don Quixote, The Odyssey,* and *Huckleberry Finn,* in addition to *Don Juan,* are also works of enchantment that simultaneously reject enchantment. All of them create a language which, in Marthe Robert's description of *Don Quixote,* is both "invocation and critique"—indeed, Alter applies this phrase to the self-conscious novel as a tradition. What may be new, however, is the anxiety created by novels like *V.* and *The Magus* in their skeptical and modernistic perspective on the daimonic. That anxiety— our uncertainty about how we are meant to take the daimonic—is the source of the suspense in such works. In *Lolita,* the comedy considerably mitigates this anxiety; it is, however, produced to an extent by the dizzying narcissism of Kinbote in *Pale Fire* and, even more, by the celebratory tone of *Ada,* that incestuous love story with a happy ending.

Writing of Spenser, Harry Berger, Jr., has said that advertised artificiality in Renaissance art functioned to mark off an area in which artist and audience could legitimately indulge their imaginations. Today similar techniques of self-consciousness serve to keep our imaginations in check by telling us that what we are offered is only a fiction, merely a myth. Yet these cautionary measures, even when—as in *V.*—they seem to constitute the major theme of the work, may, once again, serve chiefly to allow us to enter a daimonic universe with a minimum of guilt and embarrassment. In sophisticated art we can consent to romance only after it has been debunked for us.

In *The Magus,* Fowles tells a fable of a young man who learns that the only way to avoid being victimized by magical illusions is to be a magician oneself. This is also true of Nabokov. In *Invitation to a Beheading,* everyone in Cincinnatus's totalitarian society appears to him to be a parody, a shadow of a reality, a copy. To be a parodist is one way of not being a parody. In *Despair,* Hermann, who seeks originality and hates and shuns mirrors, falls prey to a fake doubleness; Kinbote and Humbert are also trapped by reflections and doubles. But uniqueness resides in being able to manipulate doubleness; the inability to do this seems to be one of Nabokov's central criticisms of his failed artists. As for *Lolita* itself, it does beyond a doubt achieve singularity; however, singularity is not, as Nabokov would have it, to transcend literary relations but to be able to hold one's own among them.

Appel points out that Jakob Gradus, the assassin of *Pale Fire,* is an anagrammatic mirror-reversal of another character in that novel, Sudarg of Bokay, described as a "mirror-maker of genius," or artist. Both death and the artist create doubles of life, and each struggles against the other. For the writer the assassin comes from many directions: previous literature, current critical standards, the expectations of the audience, the resistance of language, the writer's own self-consciousness. Nabokov has spoken of the artist as an illusionist trying to "transcend the heritage" with his bag of tricks. This is the magic of sleight-of-hand, and Nabokov is referring to matters of style, technique, and language. But we are really dealing in works such as *Lolita* with the magic of the shaman and, in this case, parody—together with the other features of a proleptic comic style—is perhaps his most powerful spell.

L_olita_

David Rampton

I have tried [elsewhere] to make a case for reading Nabokov's novels as something other than "stagings" of his "inventions," and to show that their "real plot" exists, not only in the "gaps" and "holes" of the narrative, those places where Nabokov interrupts his story and shows us the actual work-ings of his novels, but also in their ostensible content. _Invitation to a Behead-ing_ and _Bend Sinister_ can be discussed in terms of their social and political ideas; _The Gift_ is a commentary on Russian literature. These are novels which, after the image patterns have been traced and the devices explained, still make propositions about a human world and a human nature that we can isolate and examine, argue with and endorse. Nabokov, I have tried to suggest, is a committed novelist, intent on expressing certain views and dramatizing certain truths. Reading his novels we feel, not just that various precepts about the autonomy of the aesthetic artefact are being exemplified, but that a view of man is being advanced.

In the case of those novels, this kind of criticism was an attempt to fill a definite gap. With _Lolita,_ the problem is a little different. For people began arguing about it almost as soon as it appeared, and the subject of their argument was the novel's content: "view of man," "human values," "atti-tudes that inform the work"—the people who thought about literature in these terms were the ones who wrote the reviews and letters to the editor that the novel's publication provoked. Why spend a chapter going over ground already well trodden? The first critic in Frederick Crews's _The Pooh Perplex_ remarks that "our ideal in English studies is to amass as much

From _Vladimir Nabokov: A Critical Study of the Novels._ © 1984 by Cambridge Uni-versity Press.

commentary as possible upon the literary work, so as to let the world know how deeply we respect it." That is a reason of sorts, but it also seems important now, nearly thirty years after the controversy about *Lolita* began, to reaffirm that some useful "new directions" in Nabokov criticism might be discovered by reconsidering some of the old directions that many critics now regard as dead ends. The edition in which a generation of students has been reading the novel is Alfred Appel's *The Annotated Lolita*. Wittily and provocatively, his long introduction and extremely detailed notes advance a view of Nabokov that now dominates critical discussions of his work, but which, as I have been arguing, needs substantial qualification. He insists that Humbert's desire for young girls is only the novel's "ostensible subject," that *Lolita* is only "supposedly about perversion," and that what seems like a depiction of real life is revealed for what it is when the "authorial voice" reminds us that "the characters have 'cotton-padded bodies' and are the author's puppets, that all is a fiction." He is joined by critics such as Julia Bader, who calls *Lolita* "a novel about literary originality," and claims that "The questions tackled by *Lolita* are artistic, or aesthetic, and the 'moral' dilemma is treated in aesthetic terms." Brenda Megerle asserts that "*Lolita* is about tantalization, specifically that tantalization which Nabokov finds in the aesthetic experience." Even Maurice Couturier, who had some insightful things to say about sexuality in the novel, contends that it is "first of all a poetic work having to do with the very process of poetic creation." When the "big" issues raised by the novel are perceived to be of strictly secondary importance, the attention of many Nabokov readers shifts to the smaller parts of the elaborate structure that constitutes *Lolita*. They wonder about details: does "Will Brown, Dolores, Colo.," one of the signatures in a motel register that Humbert reads as Quilty's mockery, mean "I will sodomize Dolores?" They seek out hidden parallels: Lensky in *Eugene Onegin* is "analogous" to Quilty, we are told, because both are murdered and both have "murdered the artistic ideals each author cherishes." The process of annotation promises to be a long and complex one. Appel points out one of the areas still unexplored when he observes, only half-jokingly, that his Notes "seldom comment on H. H.'s topographical observations; the field remains wide-open. A generous grant from the Guggenheim Foundation or the American Council of Learned Societies will no doubt one day enable some gentle don to retrace meticulously H. H.'s foul footsteps." The main directions of *Lolita* criticism seem to have been determined.

I hope to show in this chapter that there is still something to be gained from treating the "ostensible subject" of *Lolita* as the real one, by looking for the author, not so much in the stage effects he arranges, as in the human drama he depicts. And I want to argue that only by recognizing the primacy of the human problems in a book like *Lolita,* by admitting that its force as a work of fiction depends on our responses to these problems, can we understand just what the novel has to tell about the creative task that Nabokov has set himself. What follows is divided into three sections: (1) Nabokov's treatment of his sexual subject matter; (2) the whole question of *Lolita*'s ambiguity and the dilemmas it creates for the reader; and (3) the relation between Nabokov's aesthetics and the content of his novel.

As everyone knows, *Lolita* began life as a *succès de scandale.* Many bought the latest novel from Paris's Olympia Press thinking it was pornographic. The British government debated its merits at cabinet level and asked the French to ban its sale. It even had a certain political impact: Nigel Nicolson narrowly lost his Bournemouth seat because he publicly supported its publication. The appearance of the book in England caused some particularly violent outbursts. Looking back from our vantage point, we might well be reassured by the denunciations of *Lolita* in letters to various journals. They often express the genuine concern of people who cared about literature. Nabokov's novel is not the handbook for child molesters that some of them took it to be, but we can hardly be condescending about their anxieties. The source of them was the firm belief that the publication of a book was an important event, that a novel could actually affect people's lives.

What was not generally known at the time was that the author of *Lolita* shared many of the conservative views of his attackers in so far as the literary representation of sexual relations was concerned. In a 1946 letter to Edmund Wilson, whose *Memoirs of Hecate County* had offended the law, Nabokov offered his friend some examples of real pornography for use in the campaign to keep the novel from being banned. One is a chapter from Thomas Heggan's *Mr Roberts,* in which there is a story "about sailors looking through a telescope at nurses having showerbaths and the point of the story is a mole on one of the girls' fanny." The other is an article in the *International Digest* "about the way Eskimos copulate." It includes pictures of children imitating the actions of their parents who, says the reporter, "chuckle at their youngsters' realism." Nabokov deplored not just this kind of vulgarity but explicit sexual references in serious literature as well. Lawrence he calls "a pornographer," and even the revered *Ulysses* is criticized for its "obnoxious, overdone preoccupation with sex organs" and for the "sexual affairs" which "heap indecency upon indecency." But how is the bruise on Lolita's thigh which so fascinates Humbert in his encounter with her on the living-room sofa different from the mole that interests Heggan's sailors? And isn't *Lolita* as preoccupied with sexual affairs as *Lady Chatterley's Lover* or *Ulysses*? A comparison between Nabokov's approach to his highly charged material and those of some of the authors he criticizes will help clarify matters.

Here is a description of an orgasm, taken at random from *Lady Chatterley:* "And she quivered, and her own mind melted out. Sharp soft waves of unspeakable pleasure washed over her as he entered her, and started the curious molten thrilling that spread and spread till she was carried away with the last, blind flash of extremity." Lawrence's prose here is that of a writer who does not really care about words as such. Sex is not mental; therefore only an approximate language is available to describe it. The occasional slovenliness of the style that results is uncomfortably close to the kind of stuff that can be found in any sex shop, and this makes Nabokov's "pornographer" remark seem less absurd than it at first appears. He thought this kind of sex in fiction was crude and anti-artistic. Whatever else he does in *Lolita* Nabokov never writes like this.

The contrast with Joyce is more complex. Here is a short excerpt from *Ulysses* (Bloom is watching Gerty Macdowell):

And then a rocket sprang and bang shot blind and O! then the Roman candle burst and it was like a sigh of O! and everyone cried O! O! in raptures and it gushed out of it a stream of rain gold hair threads and they shed and ah! they were all greeny dewy stars falling with golden, O so lovely! O so soft, sweet, soft!

Then all melted away dewily in the grey air: all was silent. Ah!

Nabokov would never have written this either. In one of his novels a character with Bloom's background and interests could enjoy only a decidedly inferior kind of sexual pleasure, and there would therefore be no linguistic fireworks to record it. His skilled lovers are always aristocrats of some sort, and his commoners are copulators. (In his Joyce lectures he says that Bloom "indulges in acts and dreams that are definitely subnormal in the zoological, evolutional sense.") Besides, Nabokov could never allow language to let go in this way. Consider Humbert's Bloom-like autoerotic arrangements:

All the while keeping a maniac's inner eye on my distant golden goal, I cautiously increased the magic friction that was doing away, in an illusional, if not factual, sense, with the physically irremovable, but psychologically very friable texture of the ma-

terial divide (pajamas and robe) between the weight of two sun-
burnt legs, resting athwart my lap, and the hidden tumor of an
unspeakable passion.

Whereas Blooms' excitement is represented by the breakdown of normal
sentence patterns, and the breathless association of interjections and epi-
thets, run together with commas and coordinating conjunctions to create a
prose analogue for his experience, Humbert's is a lexical adventure, in
impeccable syntactic uniform. Joyce is intent on giving us the actual physical details of his two synchronized explosions. In Nabokov it all ends, not
with an explosion, but with what Humbert later describes as a sort of
muffled "internal combustion." More importantly, Nabokov has his hero
blend romantic hyperbole ("unspeakable passion") with a technical precision ("friable texture") that reinforces the contrast between what is happening and how it is being described. Humbert occasionally reminds us that at
the time he slipped out of mental gear, as when he recalls how he recited the
lyrics of a popular song to disguise his mounting excitement, but we are
given only bits of what we would have heard had we been there. In the text,
the nonsense verse of incipient orgasm is simply an indecorous interruption
in what has become a formal rhetorical adventure. And decorum, sexual
and syntactic, is what Humbert insists on: "anxiety forced me to work," he
says, "for the first minute or so, more hastily than was consensual with
deliberately modulated enjoyment." When ecstasy is finally imminent, he
emphasizes not frenzied abandon but order and control. He has reached
what he calls "that state of absolute security, confidence and reliance not
found elsewhere in conscious life." The elaborate formal apparatus makes
all this carnal desire different in kind from the experiences conveyed by the
authors Nabokov criticizes: even the passage from Joyce seems explicit by
comparison. If sex must be dealt with in a novel, Nabokov seems to be
saying, authors should proceed with Humbert's circumspection.

Here we seem to be on the verge of admitting that someone like Appel
is right, that sex is only what *Lolita* appears to be about, and that the
fictional form in which that subject is dealt with is what in the end should be
the principal object of the reader's attention. But look at what happens in
one of the last reported sexual encounters between Humbert and Lolita, the
one at Beardsley School:

> At one of [the desks], my Lolita was reading the chapter on
> "Dialogue" in Baker's *Dramatic Technique,* and all was very
> quiet, and there was another girl with a very naked, porcelain-
> white neck and wonderful platinum hair, who sat in front read-

ing too, absolutely lost to the world and interminably winding a soft curl around one finger, and I sat beside Dolly just behind that neck and that hair, and unbuttoned my overcoat and for sixty-five cents plus the permission to participate in the school play, had Dolly put her inky, chalky, red-knuckled hand under the desk.

There is more novelistic foregrounding here. Reading is represented as an activity that cuts people off from life, the equivalent of that "intangible island of entranced time" which Humbert imagines his nymphets inhabiting. Borges remarks that this sense of *dédoublement,* becoming aware of other people in a dramatic presentation doing what we ourselves are doing, frightens us because it suggests that we may be the characters in someone else's story, that our point of view may be part of an infinite series. Nabokov uses the same device here, but its primary effect is to involve the reader in what is being represented. By dropping a mirror in front of the scene, he does make us aware that we are reading a book, lost in a world that is now suddenly looking back at us. But he shows us two readers, an innocent and a not so innocent one. Lolita, reading a book about acting, is not so cut off from the world that the transaction cannot be agreed upon, a transaction whose sordidness is not obscured by the mirroring device. The scene's shock value is enhanced by the presence of a fourth person, a sort of spirit that presides over the action: the young girl in the reproduction of Reynolds's "Age of Innocence" which hangs above the blackboard. If we consider the title alone this may seem like overly obvious irony. However, if we recall the actual details of that painting—the kneeling figure of a young girl in a white dress, the bare neck, the soft curls, the slightly tense, abstracted gaze directed toward some point outside the frame, the dark shape and the overcast sky in the background—we realize that Nabokov has modelled his innocently unaware reader on this girl. (These effects would have been appreciated by more of Nabokov's readers than one might think. Copies of Reynold's painting must have decorated many middle-class North American homes in the fifties, if the small Canadian town in which I grew up is any indication.) Of particular interest are the girl's hands, folded on her breast, right in the middle of the picture. For Nabokov "centres" the hands of his figures too, with the usual combination of closely observed detail and a prose rhythm which becomes a significant part of the description: "interminably winding a soft curl around one finger" is appropriately sinuous, and "inky, chalky, red-knuckled" a wonderful example of how a different set of consonants can help to recreate a very different hand. The result for the reader then is a complex double awareness: human life and fictional analogues, the consequences of desire along with the devices of the novelist, the defilement of a precious image which is magnified by a subtle allusion. The intricacies of the style do not conceal what is actually happening under cover of overcoats and ellipses, and Nabokov succeeds in showing us just how shocking subtlety and restraint can be. This then is a good example of how he brings his "ostensible" subject to life, in a scene that is neither simple literary artifice nor pornography, but part of a study of pornography, of how power and desire instrumentalize people.

Yet even the effect of this scene is not unequivocal. Humbert is with Lolita here because he has just survived an interview with the rather horrible headmistress, Miss Pratt, during which he solicits our sympathy by calling himself "a cornered old rat," and by toying with the idea of marrying and strangling his inquisitor. The classroom masturbation session is reported by someone we have just been siding with. Clearly the issue of how sex is portrayed by *Lolita* is part of a larger problem. The book cries out for a condemnation, a defence, a judgment, yet for various reasons it actively subverts the judgment-making capacity of the reader. Anyone committed to determining the author's position in regard to the events represented must sooner or later come to terms with the fact that a great deal of *Lolita* works at denying him the very certainty he is seeking. He may even start to wonder just why he is so sure that the novel's moral recommendations ought to be clearly and coherently manifest, why he is so eager to find out "the truth" and pronounce sentence upon it.

One way out of the dilemma is to decide that *Lolita*'s ambiguities and the doubts they create are the product of a naïve reading which the novel itself challenges the reader to move beyond. Solemnly discussing a playful writer's improvised creations as if they were real people becomes, if he chooses this option, the kind of response that recent critical advances have thoroughly discredited. Here is Appel again:

> If one responds to the author's "false scents" and "specious lines
> of play," best effected by parody, and believes, say, that Humbert's confession is "sincere" and that he exorcises his guilt, . . .
> or that a Nabokov book is an illustration of a reality proceeding
> under the natural laws of our world—then one has not only lost
> the game to the author, but most likely is not faring too well in
> the "game of worlds," one's own unscrambling of pictures.

Yet this seemingly sophisticated response threatens to oversimplify matters considerably. Why, we might ask, can't the naïve reader and the critical reader inhabit the same body? And if the naïve reader, with his assumptions about the embodiment of a world in *Lolita* that is mediated by but not supplanted by language, has been defeated by the author, where then are the novel's tension and complexity, its power to disorient and disconcert? Lionel Trilling confesses at the end of his article on *Lolita* that one of its chief attractions is "its ambiguity of tone . . . and its ambiguity of intention, its ability to arouse uneasiness, to throw the reader off balance, to require him to change his stance and shift his position and move on." But he could not have felt this unless he took *Lolita* to be in some sense "an illusion of a reality proceeding under the natural laws of our world." Instead of alerting us to the novel's problematic nature, Appel's dismissal threatens to banish it at a stroke. The literary self-consciousness that he stresses here is crucially important, but only because it involves the reader in a complex range of responses.

Let us consider some specific examples from the novel with a view to defining how the problem posed by parody and irony in *Lolita* might best be approached. Here is Humbert's account of his reaction at the scene of Charlotte's fatal accident:

> The widower, a man of exceptional self-control, neither wept nor raved. He staggered a bit, that he did; but he opened his mouth only to impart such information or issue such directions as were strictly necessary in connection with the identification, examination and disposal of a dead woman, the top of her head a porridge of bone, brains, bronze hair and blood.

That is, faced with the task of summarizing his response to an appalling spectacle and the violent death of someone he knew well, Humbert parodies a newspaper account and "identifies" the gory remains of his wife with a cadenza of repeated consonants. One of *Lolita*'s reviewers was not so much disconcerted by this passage as outraged by it. In his *Spectator* review, Kingsley Amis cites parallels between Humbert's confession and Nabokov's autobiography, comparing both their interest in young girls by the seaside and their stylistic predilections, and argues that Nabokov endorses the cruelty and insensitivity that he portrays in the novel. He then quotes the above passage and appends a sardonic: "That's the boy, Humbert/Nabokov, alliterative to the last." Of course there is a sense in which this identification is correct. Nabokov dislikes the Charlottes of this world, and getting her out of the way is as important for him as it is for Humbert: narrative and libidinous interests here coincide. And although he doesn't say it explicitly, Amis alerts us to something even more important, something often overlooked by critics more sympathetic to what Nabokov is trying to do. His comment reminds us that there is something profoundly disintegrative in Nabokov's sensibility that makes him write novel after novel about the various ways in which human beings go about destroying themselves. Yet it is the combination of violence and contempt on the one hand and gentleness and compassion on the other that makes Nabokov and his heroes so interesting. Charlotte's death scene is no exception. For the most striking thing about the whole range of Humbert's responses to her timely demise is that the language he uses points, not just to itself by virtue of things like alliteration, but to all those emotions which exist beyond language and can only be hinted at, and yet are in this oblique way effectively conveyed.

The main problem for the reader seems to be deciding how relevant a criterion like "sincerity" is when one is dealing with an intensely self-conscious rhetorical style, and what kind of authority is given to a particular view by the context. Here is another example of the Humbert style in action: "I had always thought that wringing one's hands was a fictional gesture—the outcome, perhaps, of some medieval ritual; but as I took to the woods, for a spell of despair and desperate meditation, this was the gesture ('look, Lord, at these chains!') that would have come nearest to the mute expression of my mood." This kind of passage reminds us how often Humbert indulges in just this kind of "fictional" gesture. Ten minutes with the text reveals six variations of "monster," plus "ape," "bestial," "brute," "Mr Hyde," "shameful vice" and "foul lust." For most readers these sessions of passionate self-mortification are genuinely perplexing: so much talk about guilt now that it is too late for anything but talk, and yet it is precisely the Humbert "talk," the marvellously intelligent discourse that devastatingly indicts not just himself but a whole society, that makes him so attractive and keeps us sympathetic and involved. This is of course not a new problem. In his penchant for culpatory effusion Humbert joins a long line of guilty heroes, a whole literary tradition in fact, forcefully though somewhat uncharitably summed up by Wyndham Lewis in some remarks about the nineteenth-century decadents from whom Nabokov's hero has inherited some of his tastes and affectations: Lewis notes "the astonishing role played by morals" in what he calls "this spectacle of calculated perversity" and adds:

> Byron, Wilde, Huysmans (that is to say—incest, pederasty and homicide)—what is that, at bottom, but the good old melodrama of *The Girl Who Took the Wrong Turning?* . . . Here surely is an object lesson, if one were needed, in the disadvantages of

> an excessive development of the ethical will: for by the simple
> expedient of reversing it, it can be converted into a first-class
> instrument of farcical self-display, with all the army of false
> values that marches upon the heels of such an operation.

Humbert's "farcical self-display" certainly leaves him open to this kind of criticism, but the literary nature of his self-consciousness changes the game considerably. A hero who Byronizes is one thing; one who tries out the role of handsome, moody, ill-starred protagonist while keeping up a running commetary on the literary precedents, is quite another. How are we to pin down such a well-read hero and refute the notion that *Lolita*'s readers are trapped in a world that is bounded on all sides by literature?

A look at some passages in which explicit literary parody is the vehicle for Humbert's self-conscious declamations may provide some tentative answers. Consider the scene in which he ponders the implications of Charlotte's marriage proposal and then does an impromptu imitation of Dostoyevski's Underground Man: "After a while I destroyed the letter and went to my room, and ruminated, and rumpled my hair, and modeled my purple robe, and moaned through clenched teeth and suddenly—Suddenly, gentlemen of the jury, I felt a Dostoyevskian grin dawning (through the very grimace that twisted my lips) like a distant and terrible sun." In this scene I think we are meant to feel that Humbert is still very much in control of the language and the parody, and the effect is primarily comic. "That may be all very well for Dostoyevski," he is saying, "but my emotional turmoil will not be expressed so glibly." The conventional nature of Dostoyevski's torments and revelations is exposed, and the arbitrary nature of Humbert's task, the freedom he enjoys in deciding how he will report what has happened, is subtly conveyed to the reader. Yet we know, even if Nabokov doesn't want to admit it, that his hero is intimately related to Dostoyevski's heroes, who are in turn part of a long tradition of "superfluous men" in nineteenth-century Russian literature. Just below the passage Nabokov is alluding to in *Notes from Underground,* the one in which the Underground Man, in his bathrobe, confronts the woman who loves him, we find this:

> And all at once I burst into tears. It was a real fit of hysteria. I
> was hot with shame, but I could not restrain my sobs . . . "Wa-
> ter, give me some water—over there!" I muttered feebly, con-
> scious, however, that I could quite well do without water, or
> feeble mutterings either. I was *putting on an act,* as they call it, to

preserve the decencies, even though my hysteria was genuine enough.

Like Humbert, the Underground Man knows that his hysteria is spurious in the sense that it is the result of his self-dramatizing propensities; but he has come to realize that the same could be said about everything he does—hence his "genuine" hysteria. In other words, he is as self-aware as one of Nabokov's heroes. And standing behind him is someone like Stavrogin who, again like Humbert, is at one point confronted by the ghost of a little girl he has "killed." The emotional resonance of this kind of antecedent looms up as soon as Dostoyevski is mentioned in *Lolita*. Even when Nabokov rejects his predecessors, as he does Dostoyevski, for what he considers their false values and their melodrama, he ends up rewriting and extending their stories.

Literary figures haunt *Lolita* right to the end, and their effects are just as complex. The murder of Quilty is a good example. Humbert's approach to "Pavor Manor" is an imitation of the opening of Poe's "The Fall of the House of Usher," yet the parodic effect is only intermittent: Nabokov has other things on his mind. Besides, Poe's narrator suffers from an "utter depression of soul" which he compares to "the after-dream of the reveller upon opium—the bitter lapse into everyday life—the hideous dropping off of the veil . . . an iciness, a sinking, a sickening of the heart—an unredeemed dreariness of thought which no goading of the imagination could torture into aught of the sublime"; and you cannot say fairer than that. Obliged to sustain the dramatic interest of a crucial scene, reluctant to interrupt his narrative with a distracting tour de force, Nabokov settles for parodic echoes only, a few details about the house, a little phone "atmosphere." The other literary presence in this scene is T. S. Eliot: Quilty's versified death sentence is, in part, a comic version of *Ash-Wednesday*. The distinctive repetitions of the first section of the poem positively cry out for parodic imitation:

> Because you took advantage of a sinner
> because you took advantage
> because you took
> because you took advantage of my disadvantage

Nabokov has some fun with what he regards as Eliot's pomposities, yet even as comic imitation the lines retain a kind of force that simple burlesque would not. They are funny, but they ring true. Significantly, Nabokov leaves Eliot in the next lines and mocks his own hero:

>Because you took advantage of a sin
>when I was helpless moulting moist and tender
>hoping for the best
>dreaming of marriage in a mountain state
>aye of a litter of Lolitas

Surely this is the sentimental Humbert, out of control, being mocked by his creator for his *Stuffed Owl* style. Emotion spills onto the page, not as emotion but as clichés. Eliot's rhythms and diction turn up only occasionally after this ("the awfulness of love and violets / remorse despair"); and the poem, after summarizing Humbert's patently self-serving views on Quilty's responsibility for everything that has happened, takes yet another turn near the end and actually manages to create some more pathos, in lines such as "took a dull doll to pieces / and threw its head away." Why has a small part of Eliot's poem been grafted onto this hybrid? If we try to account for its presence by pointing out that *Lolita* is the story of a sinner at the hour of his death, or about the "torment / Of love unsatisfied" and "The greater torment / Of love satisfied," then it seems that we must take credit for isolating these lines, since Nabokov has nothing specific to say about them. Still, they are there in the background, providing a kind of resonance that we cannot ignore. The passage sustains its effect by using its literary antecedents to go beyond the literary.

So does Humbert "exorcize his guilt?" Does Nabokov make clear how his hero is to be judged? Some critics insist that he never does reveal himself, e.g., Brenda Megerle: "the novel offers no authorial judgment of Humbert's actions." Others work at identifying the various elements of the hero's highly self-conscious discourse, and then try to decide when the reader is right to take him straight. Thus Nomi Tamir-Ghez, at the end of an article describing the rhetorical devices Humbert uses to manipulate the reader and justify his own actions, claims: "It is his self-castigation, his readiness to face and admit his guilt, and his suffering at the realization of the truth, that make us accept him. At the end of the narrative he at last gives up the cynicism underlying his rhetoric, and his tone becomes more sincere." I think she is essentially right, but those who share Lewis's suspicions about the self-indulgent aspects of all that confessing are still not answered. Nor are those who wonder why Humbert's cynicism should stop here: what allows us to assume that he has not arranged this "sincerity" in one last attempt to dupe the unsuspecting reader?

My sense is that the best answer is provided by the least rhetorical parts of the novel: the dramatized scenes, in which the reader, less distracted than usual by Humbert's syntax and diction, can listen to words that were actually said, forgetting for a moment that even these can be manipulated by an unreliable narrator. Humbert's last meeting with Lolita is one such scene. It is as close as the novel comes to what would be the moment of the hero's conversion in a tragedy, though perhaps "conversion" is not exactly the right word. After all, Humbert leaves Coalmont just as intent on killing Quilty as he was when he came. But there is a real change, one that involves the reader's perceptions of him as much as anything else. For the scene opens with Humbert in his role as executioner, dressed in black, gun in hand, croaking "Husband at home?" his first words for Lolita, whom he hasn't seen for three years. In other words, we are seeing him at his most vile, all ready for a gruesome slaughter while the wife of his victim looks on, and he makes no attempt to hide this from us. By the time he has finished narrating this scene, he is making an impassioned plea for his love and repudiating his "sterile and selfish vice." The contrast could not be more complete. The whole episode loses much of its dramatic point if we do not finally believe in this love, but Nabokov does not make it easy for us. Appel remarks on "the parodic echo of Billy Graham's exhortation" when Humbert pleads with Lolita to come away with him ("Make those twenty-five steps. Now"), and the "purposeful banality" of "And we shall live happily ever after." Even at its most lyrical, his prose can take some unexpectedly crude turns, as when he describes Lolita as "the faint violet whiff and dead leaf echo of the nymphet I had rolled myself upon." Those who want to believe in a reformed Humbert can point to the compelling simplicity with which he describes his feelings, a sharp contrast to the fulsome quality of his earlier declarations. Faced with someone who is "hopelessly worn at seventeen," i.e., long past nymphet age, he says "I looked and looked at her, and knew as clearly as I know I am to die, that I loved her more than anything I had ever seen or imagined on earth, or hoped for anywhere else."

It is easier to believe this, and to see his love as somehow ennobling, if we are convinced that it is no longer being lavished on an illusory object. Here we have to forget about rhetorical devices and compounded ironies for a moment and ask whether Nabokov wants us to believe in a changed Lolita as well. I think he does, although he has only this one scene to show how the twelve-year-old girl so clearly established in our minds has changed into a more mature and more reflective young woman. The first part of their conversation makes that conviction seem rather sentimental. After all, how much older and wiser is someone who still thinks Quilty is "a great guy in many respects"? Although this is admittedly grotesque, Nabokov's reluctance to violate psychological realism makes such sentiments both plausible and necessary. Because of her arrested emotional development, Lolita will always idolize Quilty. He still represents the possibility of escape for her. But even her life with him has an unreal quality for her now, and the rest of the conversation with Humbert suggests just how much she has learned from the past and how far she has put it behind her. He insists on knowing what went on at Quilty's ranch, but she is reluctant to reply, probably because she thinks he is up to his old voyeuristic tricks. But he isn't. Rather, he wants to suffer, and for that he needs explicit details. Besides, killing Quilty will be sweeter if Humbert knows exactly what he is taking revenge for. Lolita mentions "weird, filthy, fancy things," but this is not enough for him:

> "What things exactly?"
> "Oh, things . . . Oh, I—really I"—she uttered the "I" as a subdued cry while she listened to the source of the ache, and for lack of words spread the five fingers of her angularly up-and-down-moving hand. No, she gave it up, she refused to go into particulars with that baby inside her.

This is one of the finest moments in the book. The movement of the hand (Nabokov is always watching the hands of his characters) captures the whole nature of Lolita's predicament. Her sense of right and wrong is all the more moving because it is not in her power to say why she cannot tell. This refusal, taken together with her refusal to go along with Quilty's demands or to agree to what she (mistakenly) thinks Humbert is offering her when he asks her to go with him, requires us to reexamine our assumptions about her. Nabokov has already subtly misdirected these assumptions. As Humbert watches Lolita smoke a cigarette, he is struck by a resemblance: "Gracefully, in a blue mist, Charlotte Haze rose from her grave." The implication is that Lolita is in the process of becoming another Charlotte, another cipher in mindless America. The tawdriness of Coalmont, the photo of the in-laws, the radio "singing of folly and fate" all help create this impression. But in the midst of all this Lolita stands out as somehow different. A young Charlotte would be more harsh and bitter, a jaded teenager, old and wise before her time. Her daughter's bemused reflectiveness ("It was so *strange*, so *strange*") seems to hint at another future. During a first reading of the novel, this future is still very much at issue. By the time the reader learns that she is "Mrs Richard Schiller," he has probably long since forgotten what Dr John Ray says in the Foreword about the "Mrs Richard F. Schiller" who "died in childbed, giving birth to a stillborn girl." Her rejection of Humbert's offer of an escape may condemn her to a life of drudgery, but in committing herself to a husband and a baby she is making the only human choice available to her. Humbert understands this. His love is devastatingly unrequited but he sees its object clearly. And Nabokov, in this one scene, shows us all the poignancy of Lolita's attempt to build a future for herself in a world that was not of her making. Such a scene doesn't "solve" the problem of *Lolita;* the issues raised by the novel are not the kind that anyone ever solves. But it does remind us why *Lolita* matters and why we go on talking about it.

Any attempt to discuss a novel of Nabokov's in terms of "human values" must inevitably come to terms with the fact that he usually insisted that a novel's aesthetic values were preeminent in his mind while writing it, and that in general as an author aesthetic values were all he ever cared about. To an interviewer who asked him about the function of his novels he said: "I have no purpose at all when composing my stuff except to compose it. I work hard, I work long, on a body of words until it grants me complete possession and pleasure." His well-known remark in the Afterword to *Lolita* expresses the same sentiments: "For me," he writes, "a work of fiction exists only insofar as it affords me what I shall bluntly call aesthetic bliss, that is a sense of being somehow, somewhere, connected with other states of being where art (curiosity, tenderness, kindness, ecstasy) is the norm." I want to suggest in this final section that the human drama in the novel is itself an extended commentary on this question of the aesthetics of the pure artist. This sounds suspiciously like the "*Lolita* as aesthetic allegory" criticism that I was quarrelling with earlier, but it differs in this sense: rather than exemplifying the truth of precepts like the ones just quoted, *Lolita,* I want to argue, offers a less doctrinaire and more complex view of the subject than Nabokov's own comments generally do.

Like his creator, Humbert is preeminently concerned with "aesthetic bliss." Here he is on the subject of Lolita's tennis:

> I remember at the very first game I watched being drenched with an almost painful convulsion of beauty assimilation. My Lolita had a way of raising her bent left knee at the ample and springy start of the service cycle when there would develop and hang in the sun for a second a vital web of balance between toed foot, pristine armpit, burnished arm and far back-flung racket, as she smiled up with gleaming teeth at the small globe suspended so high in the zenith of the powerful and graceful cosmos she had created for the express purpose of falling upon it with a clean resounding crack of her golden whip.

"Gleaming teeth" sounds like a toothpaste commercial, and a tennis ball leaves the racket with a sound that is less thin and less cruel than the "crack" of a whip, but otherwise, how brilliantly this account freezes and immortalizes its subject. Notice the way Nabokov, in the second sentence, delays the subject of the second clause and thus imitates in prose the suspension he is describing. The spondee-like "so high" has a similar effect, and the phrases that release the tension created form a brisk combination of iambs and anapests. Even if Humbert had made home movies ("Idiot, triple idiot! I could have filmed her!"), they would have been superseded by these sentences which take Lolita frame by frame through her subtle and elegant ritual. Humbert's "aesthetic bliss" is a lot like Nabokov's: he too claims that the contemplation of the aesthetic object creates in the observer a sense of "other states of being," what he calls "the teasing delirious feeling of teetering on the very brink of unearthly order and splendor." This idea of discovering a hidden harmony by contemplating the Beautiful is of course not original with Humbert. It was a favourite of the symbolists, and in matters of aesthetics both he and Nabokov often sound like one of them. Nabokov's most intimate link with this movement was with the Russian symbolists, whose work he knew well even as a youth. A poem like Blok's "The Stranger" or some of the passages devoted to Lyudmila in Sologub's *The Petty Demon* could almost serve as sources for the hero's fascination in *Lolita* with the body of the woman he loves. Vaguely evil, frightening, tantalizing, inspiring, all the time hinting at other, more perfect realms— Lolita is very much a creation born of this tradition. I don't want to push the parallel between Humbert and Nabokov too far; yet if there is a correspondence between the general aesthetic views being expressed here, then *Lolita,* to the extent that it is a study of the effects of holding such views, should have something useful to tell us about Nabokov's own art and about the tradition he inherited.

The novel offers one explicit comment on this question. It takes the form of Humbert's summing up of his own quest for beauty, at the moment when the narrative pauses between his last meeting with Lolita and the encounter with Quilty. In a small "dead-of-night" town, Humbert thinks about what he has done. Nabokov suggests the symbolic implications of the setting by having him remind us that he is between Coalmont and Ramsdale: that is, between a town that epitomizes the bleakness Lolita will have to fight against, a town so grey "You can't see the morons for the smog," and a town that represents the comfortable banality of the past and the home that he has deprived her of. The nameless, silent place where Humbert stops is a piece of quintessential Americana for Nabokov. Not oppressive or alienating or inhuman, ideal for "dark night of the soul" thoughts about isolation and death, but depressing because of its emptiness and vaguely unreal quality. Besides, its insouciant vulgarity violates the aesthetic sense. From his car Humbert can see a "large thermometer with the name of a laxative" on the front of a drugstore, a "display of artificial diamonds" reflected in the "red mirror" of a jewelry store, and the silent, comic, curiously disheartening repetition of an "animated" neon sign. The social criticism is only there by implication, but the scene does instill in the reader's mind the idea of an American "sense of beauty," a point that will be important for an understanding of what Humbert is about to say. (For those expecting some Old World nostalgia here, Nabokov has a characteristic feint, the unexpected adjective at the end of a conventional series: "Nobody strolled and laughed on the sidewalks as relaxing burghers would in sweet, mellow, rotting Europe," says Humbert.) As he reviews the past he realizes that he will always be tormented by his conscience, because he will always be guilty of having robbed Lolita of her childhood, and concludes:

> I see nothing for the treatment of my misery but the melancholy and very local palliative of articulate art. To quote an old poet:
>
> > The moral sense in mortals is the duty
> > We have to pay on mortal sense of beauty.

What does this mean exactly? Martin Green offers a useful paraphrase:

> The consolations of religion and the rigors of mortality are both derived from the aesthetic sense. What is beautiful is so because it satisfies our moral sense among other things, but the idea of beauty is the larger. The moral sense is an obligation, which we pay resignedly as a part of the price of beauty. This duty is not Kantianly near to religion; it is nearer to Customs and Excise.

But does this fit the facts? Is Humbert's sense of beauty responsible for his pangs of conscience? We know that his aesthetic sensibility was finely tuned when he had no moral sense at all, when he was still the pure embodiment of selfishness and self-indulgence, when he thought that a lecher was an "artist" and sex offenders were "poets." Humbert may want us to believe that the "moral sense" is a late stage in the life cycle of the aesthetic instinct, but his own story seems to suggest that the two things develop independently of each other.

I think the situation is clarified if we realize that two different conceptions of art are involved. Humbert's "sense of beauty" begins as pure aestheticism: he defines his problems in aesthetic terms; he yearns for a private world constructed according to exclusively aesthetic criteria. His story records the consequences of trying to live in such a world. For Nabokov too there is a dual conception at work. The novelist begins his task with certain technical problems in mind. His novel resembles, as Nabokov said about *Lolita,* a "riddle" with an "elegant solution." But the feeling it produces in the end is more than just the sense of satisfaction that results from having successfully negotiated various artistic difficulties. Take another look at his definition of "aesthetic bliss," in particular his defining "art" with nouns like "curiosity, tenderness, ecstasy." These words hint at the kind of emotional and moral commitment involved in what he regards as the ideal relation between the observer and the aesthetic object. *Lolita* is more than an impersonal artefact which gave its creator a certain amount of pleasure in the making, because it dramatizes the potential inhumanity of the kind of aesthetic attitude to experience that fails to make this kind of commitment. But it doesn't simply express a preference for warm and vital human beings as opposed to cold and impersonal works of art. Humbert's description of Lolita at tennis is an exercise in the special art of seeing her as an object, an art that only aesthetic detachment makes possible. And his "Confession," the product of that detachment, is at the same time a study of its limitations. As Michael Bell points out in "*Lolita* and Pure Art," it is not "that the awareness of others as 'objects' is in itself wrong, but that it has to find its proper place in our general sense of them."

The correspondence between what Humbert finds out about the pursuit of beauty and what *Lolita* tells us about Nabokov's own aesthetics can be taken a stage farther. No one can read the last part of the novel without feeling the hectic urgency of the narrative: the aimless pursuits, the dead ends, the night journeys to nowhere, the increasingly oppressive sense of solitude. Trying to find and kill Quilty means trying to make a sinister "second self" responsible for what has happened, to isolate evil in a fundamentally narcissistic and unreal way. The search for that self is a waste of time. Humbert achieves nothing during the three years that he is away from Lolita; and looking back on these years, he realizes that his entire life has been little more than a large-scale version of them. He is forty-two years old and has left no evidence of his existence, done nothing that is of any use to anyone. He undertakes his story as a search for a "private self," that very literary exercise with all the gloomy metaphors about probing dark areas and illuminating hidden depths. But by the time he is finished, he is reconciled to the fact that it is his public self, the record of what he has contributed and accomplished, by which he will ultimately be judged. He will be whatever his readers, the collective body to whom he appeals at the end, finally decide that he is. For all his talk about the artistic abilities of the nympholept, Humbert never really creates anything until he understands that the artist requires an audience, however dimly projected, if the circuit of communication is to function properly. He has no exalted notions about the kind of immortality he will gain by writing *Lolita*. Art is not a miracle cure for mortality, a fact he wryly acknowledges in his penultimate sentence about "aurochs and angels" and "the refuge of art." Angels escaped extinction by taking refuge in literature; the aurochs, a species of wild ox that formerly inhabited Europe, has vanished forever. Humbert hopes that a part-time beast, and former inhabitant of Europe, can imitate the angels and escape into literature too.

What about the parallel with Nabokov? Despite all he said about the self-sufficiency of the author's "aesthetic bliss," he too cared about how his work would be received. In letters to Edmund Wilson written when "the *Lolita* affair" was beginning, he twice confesses to being "depressed" by the fact that some readers cannot understand that his novel is clearly not pornographic. And *Lolita* itself, despite its current reputation, constitutes his admission that the reader is not there only to be teased and tyrannized but is a vital part of a cooperative enterprise, and that aesthetic principles exist to be analyzed, tested, and refined in the product of that enterprise. Can a novel that has created such a variety of readers go on creating new ones? Will its future be gradual academic extinction, or immortality? There are, according to Borges, two kinds of classic. First there is "The Classic," the one everybody knows about but nobody reads. In this way, a masterpiece like *Don Quixote* can become, because of men's complacency and neglect, "the occasion of patriotic toasts, grammatical insolence and obscene de luxe editions." The other is the genuine classic, "that book which a nation (or group of nations, or time itself) has taken the decision to read as if in its pages everything were predetermined, predestined, deep as the cosmos, and capable of endless interpretation." *Lolita* is surely the Nabokov novel that has the best chance of becoming a classic, but it will only be the second kind if we remember that its greatness depends primarily on the human situation it portrays and on the human world it creates for us.

Chronology

1899   Vladimir Vladimirovich Nabokov is born on April 23 in St. Petersburg to the eminent jurist Vladimir Dmitrievich Nabokov and his wife, Elena Ivanovna. In 1906 Nabokov begins his lifelong affair with lepidoptery, first collecting butterflies at Vyra, the Nabokov family summer estate. Until 1911, Nabokov is educated at home by private tutors; from 1911 to 1917, he attends a progressive school in St. Petersburg. In 1916 Nabokov publishes privately his first book of poetry, a work he later disowns.

1919   The Nabokov family escapes Russia, settling eventually in Berlin. Vladimir Nabokov enters Trinity College, Cambridge, on a scholarship.

1922   Vladimir Dmitrievich is assasinated by right-wing Russian terrorists at a political rally in Berlin. Nabokov graduates from Cambridge with Honors in French and Russian literature, then joins his family in Berlin.

1922–37 Nabokov marries Vera Evseevna Slonim in 1925. Under the pen name of "Sirin" he publishes novels, short stories, poems, and chess problems in the émigré press of Berlin and Paris. The novels written during this period are *Mary* (1926), *King, Queen, Knave* (1928), *The Defense* (1929–30), *The Eye* (1930), *Glory* (1932), *Camera Obscura* (1932), *Despair* (1934), and *Invitation to a Beheading* (1935–36). Besides his literary activities, Nabokov helps support his family by teaching French, tennis, and boxing.

1934   Son Dmitri is born.

1937   Fleeing the Nazis, the Nabokovs move to Paris where Nabokov writes *The Gift* (1937–38). His English translation of *Despair* is published in London.

1940–44	With the outbreak of World War II, the Nabokovs leave France for America, sailing shortly before the fall of Paris. Nabokov teaches at Wellesley College (1941–48) and works as a Fellow of the Museum of Comparative Zoology at Harvard University (1942–48). In 1941, he publishes *The Real Life of Sebastian Knight,* his first novel written in English.
1945	Becomes an American citizen.
1947	*Bend Sinister* published in New York.
1948	Appointed Professor of Russian and European Literature at Cornell University, a position he holds until 1959.
1951	Autobiography *Conclusive Evidence* (later to be revised as *Speak, Memory*) is published in New York.
1955	Unable to find an American publisher, Nabokov allows the Olympia Press, a Parisian publishing house specializing in pornography, to bring out *Lolita.*
1956–59	As the first reviews of *Lolita* appear, a controversy erupts over whether it is pornographic literature. In 1957, excerpts from it appear in the *Anchor Review.* Nabokov publishes *Pnin.* The following year, *Lolita* is published in America, and quickly becomes a bestseller. Supported by the royalties from American publication, Nabokov retires from teaching, and he and Vera move to Montreux, Switzerland.
1962	*Pale Fire.*
1964	Nabokov's controversial annotated translation of Pushkin's *Eugene Onegin* is published and is attacked by Edmund Wilson in *The New York Review of Books,* beginning a literary feud which eventually ends their friendship.
1965	*Despair* published, thus finishing the project of "re-Englishing," alone or with collaborators, the early Russian novels *Invitation to a Beheading* (1959), *The Gift* (1963), and *The Defense* (1964).
1966	*Speak, Memory,* the revised autobiography, is published.
1969	*Ada.*
1972	*Transparent Things.*
1973	*A Russian Beauty and Other Stories.*
1974	*Look at the Harlequins!*
1977	Dies on July 2 in Montreux while working on a novel provisionally entitled *The Original of Laura.*
1986	*The Enchanter* published, as translated by Nabokov's son Dmitri from the 1939 manuscript.

Contributors

HAROLD BLOOM, Sterling Professor of the Humanities at Yale University, is the author of *The Anxiety of Influence, Poetry and Repression,* and many other volumes of literary criticism. His forthcoming study, *Freud: Transference and Authority,* attempts a full-scale reading of all of Freud's major writings. A MacArthur Prize Fellow, he is general editor of five series of literary criticism published by Chelsea House. During 1987–88, he was appointed Charles Eliot Norton Professor of Poetry at Harvard University.

LIONEL TRILLING was University Professor at Columbia University and one of the most eminent American critics of the century. His books include *The Liberal Imagination: Essays on Literature and Society, Beyond Culture: Essays on Literature and Learning,* and *Sincerity and Authenticity.*

MARTIN GREEN is Professor of English at Tufts University. He is the author of fourteen volumes of literary and cultural criticism, including *The von Richtofen Sisters* and *The Great American Adventure.*

ALFRED APPEL, JR., Professor of English at Northwestern University, is the author of *Signs of Life, Nabokov's Dark Cinema* and the editor of *The Annotated Lolita.*

JULIA BADER teaches English at the University of California at Berkeley. She is the author of *Crystal Land: Artifice in Nabokov's English Novels.*

MICHAEL BELL is Professor of English at the University of Warwick. He is the author of *Primitivism,* a history of Canadian painting, and *The Sentiment of Reality: Truth of Feeling in the European Novel.*

THOMAS R. FROSCH is Professor of English at Queens College of the City University of New York. He is the author of *The Awakening of Albion: The Renovation of the Body in the Poetry of William Blake* and *Plum Gut,* a book of verse.

DAVID RAMPTON is the author of *Vladimir Nabokov: A Critical Study of the Novels.*

Bibliography

Aldridge, A. Owen. "*Lolita* and *Les Liaisons Dangereuses.*" *Wisconsin Studies in Contemporary Literature* 2, no. 3 (1961): 20–26.

Bruss, Elizabeth. "Vladimir Nabokov: Illusions of Reality and the Reality of Illusions." In *Autobiographical Acts: The Changing Situation of a Literary Genre,* 127–62. Baltimore: The Johns Hopkins University Press, 1976.

Butler, Diane. "*Lolita* Lepidoptera." In New World Writing, vol. 16, edited by Stewart Richardson and Corlies M. Smith, 58–84. New York: Lippincott, 1960.

Cancogni, Annapaola. "'My Sister, Do You Still Recall?': Chateaubriand/Nabokov." *Comparative Literature* 35, no. 2 (1983): 140–66.

de Rougemont, Denis. "*Lolita,* or Scandal." In *Love Declared,* translated by Richard Howard, 48–59. New York: Pantheon, 1963.

Fiedler, Leslie. *Love and Death in the American Novel,* 325–28, 400. New York: Criterion Books, 1960.

Harold, Brent. "*Lolita:* Nabokov's Critique of Aloofness." *Papers on Language and Literature* 11 (1975): 71–82.

Jones, David L. "Dolorès Disparue." *Symposium* 20 (1966): 135–40.

Josipovici, G. D. "*Lolita:* Parody and the Pursuit of Beauty." *Critical Quarterly* 6 (1964): 35–48.

Levine, Robert J. "*Lolita* and the Originality of Style." *Essays in Literature* 4 (1977): 110–21.

Mitchell, Charles. "Mythic Seriousness in *Lolita.*" *Texas Studies in Literature and Language* 5 (1963): 329–43.

Morgan, P. B. "Nabokov and Dante: The Use of *La Vita Nuova* in *Lolita.*" *Delta,* no. 17 (1983): 53–60.

Moynahan, Julian. "*Lolita* and Related Memories." *Tri-quarterly* 17, no. 1 (1970): 247–52.

Nabokov, Vladimir. *The Annotated Lolita,* edited by Alfred Appel. New York: McGraw-Hill, 1970.

Packman, David. "*Lolita:* Detection and Desire." In *Vladimir Nabokov: The Structures of Literary Desire,* 23–45. Columbia: University of Missouri Press, 1982.

Pearce, Richard. "Dislocation in Nabokov's Black (Hole) Humor: *Lolita* and *Pale Fire.*" In *The Novel in Motion: An Approach to Modern Fiction,* 66–82. Columbus: Ohio State University Press, 1983.

Proffer, Carl R. *Keys to Lolita*. Bloomington: Indiana University Press, 1968.

Rampton, David. "*Lolita*." In *Vladimir Nabokov: A Critical Study of the Novels*, 101–22. Cambridge: Cambridge University Press, 1984.

Robbe-Grillet, Alain. "La notion d'itinéraire dans *Lolita*." *L'Arc* 24 (1964): 37–38.

Roth, Phyllis A. "In Search of Aesthetic Bliss: A Rereading of *Lolita*." *College Literature* 2 (1975): 28–49.

Rowe, William W. "*Lolita*." In *Nabokov's Spectral Dimension*, 67–73. Ann Arbor: Ardis, 1981.

Scheid, Mark. "Epistemological Structures in *Lolita*." *Rice University Studies* 61, no. 1 (1975): 127–40.

Schroeter, J. "Detective Stories and Aesthetic Bliss in Nabokov." *Delta*, no. 17 (1983): 23–32.

Schultz, N. F. "Characters (Contra Characterization) in the Modern Novel." In *The Theory of the Novel*, edited by J. Halperin, 147–54. New York: Oxford University Press, 1974.

Schuman, Samuel. "*Lolita*—Novel and Screenplay." *College Literature* 5 (1978): 195–204.

Tamir-Ghez, Nomi. "The Art of Persuasion in Nabokov's *Lolita*." *Poetics Today* 1, nos. 1–2 (1979): 65–83.

Winston, Matthew. "*Lolita* and the Dangers of Fiction." *Twentieth Century Literature* 21 (1975): 421–27.

Acknowledgments

"The Last Lover: Vladimir Nabokov's *Lolita*" by Lionel Trilling from *Speaking of Literature and Society* by Lionel Trilling, © 1958 by Lionel Trilling, © 1980 by Diana Trilling and James Trilling. Reprinted by permission of Harcourt Brace Jovanovich, Inc. This essay originally appeared in *Encounter* 11, no. 4 (October 1958).

"Tolstoy and Nabokov: The Morality of *Lolita*" (originally entitled "The Morality of *Lolita*") by Martin Green from *The Kenyon Review* 28, no. 3 (June 1982), © 1966 by Kenyon College. Reprinted by permission.

"*Lolita*: The Springboard of Parody" by Alfred Appel, Jr. from *Nabokov: The Man and His Work,* edited by L. S. Dembo, © 1967 by the Regents of the University of Wisconsin. Reprinted by permission of the University of Wisconsin Press.

"*Lolita*: The Quest for Ecstasy" by Julia Bader from *Crystal Land: Artifice in Nabokov's English Novels* by Julia Bader, © 1972 by the Regents of the University of California. Reprinted by permission of the University of California Press.

"*Lolita* and Pure Art" by Michael Bell from *Essays in Criticism* 24, no. 2 (April 1974), © 1974 by Stephen Wall. Reprinted by permission of the editors of *Essays in Criticism*.

"Parody and Authenticity in *Lolita*" by Thomas R. Frosch from *Nabokov's Fifth Arc,* edited by J. E. Rivers and Charles Nicol, © 1982 by the University of Texas Press. Reprinted by permission.

"*Lolita*" by David Rampton from *Vladimir Nabokov: A Critical Study of the Novels* by David Rampton, © 1984 by Cambridge University Press. Reprinted by permission.

Index

DATE

ILL
12-7-95